AN INTRODUCTION TO UNIVERSITY GOVERNANCE

An Introduction to
UNIVERSITY GOVERNANCE

Cheryl Foy

An Introduction to University Governance
© Irwin Law, 2021

All rights reserved. No part of this publication may be reproduced, stored in a retrieval system, or transmitted, in any form or by any means, without the prior written permission of the publisher or, in the case of photocopying or other reprographic copying, a licence from Access Copyright (Canadian Copyright Licensing Agency), 56 Wellesley St W, Suite 320, Toronto, ON, M5S 2S3.

Published in 2021 by
Irwin Law Inc
Suite 206, 14 Duncan Street
Toronto, ON   M5H 3G8

www.irwinlaw.com

ISBN: 978-1-55221-575-3 | e-book ISBN: 978-1-55221-576-0

The views and opinions expressed in this book are those of the author. While general legal concepts are explored, no legal advice is given and readers should seek legal advice based on their individual facts and circumstances.

Library and Archives Canada Cataloguing in Publication

Title: An introduction to university governance / Cheryl Foy.
Names: Foy, Cheryl, author.
Description: Includes bibliographical references and index.
Identifiers: Canadiana (print) 20210191430 | Canadiana (ebook) 20210191481 |
    ISBN 9781552215753 (softcover) | ISBN 9781552215760 (PDF)
Subjects: LCSH: Universities and colleges — Canada — Administration.
Classification: LCC LB2341.8.C3 F69 2021 | DDC 378.1/010971—dc23

Cover photo provided by Ontario Tech University, depicting the university's reflecting pond and Energy Systems and Nuclear Science Research Centre.

Printed and bound in Canada.
2 3 4 5   25 24 23 22 21

Summary Table of Contents

PREFACE   xv

Introduction: Welcome to University Governance   1

Part One | Joining a University Board? Understanding the Commitment You Are Making   5

CHAPTER 1: What to Consider   7

CHAPTER 2: Fiduciary Duty   13

CHAPTER 3: Conflict of Interest   18

Part Two | Being Prepared: Understanding This Unique Sector   25

CHAPTER 4: A Framework for Diligence   27

CHAPTER 5: Key Internal Stakeholders: Students   34

CHAPTER 6: Key Internal Stakeholders: Faculty   46

CHAPTER 7: Key Internal Stakeholders: Administration   59

CHAPTER 8: Key External Stakeholders: Government   66

CHAPTER 9: Key External Stakeholders: Community   75

CHAPTER 10: Key External Stakeholders: Groups and Associations   82

CHAPTER 11: Unique and Essential Concepts   90

Part Three | Good Governance in Action   107

CHAPTER 12: Understanding Your University's Governance Structure   *109*

CHAPTER 13: The Roles of the Board and the Academic Governing Body   *120*

CHAPTER 14: Shared Governance   *159*

CHAPTER 15: The Board and the President   *169*

CHAPTER 16: An Overview of University Finances   *179*

CHAPTER 17: Wrapping It Up: Some Important Conclusions   *190*

BIBLIOGRAPHY   *195*

INDEX   *209*

ABOUT THE AUTHOR   *211*

Detailed Table of Contents

PREFACE *xv*

INTRODUCTION
Welcome to University Governance *1*

PART ONE | JOINING A UNIVERSITY BOARD? UNDERSTANDING THE COMMITMENT YOU ARE MAKING *5*

CHAPTER 1
What to Consider *7*

A. Why Should You Join a University Board? *7*

B. Universities Are Complex Places to Govern *8*

C. Educate Yourself About the University and Your Role *9*

Appendix 1.1 *11*

CHAPTER 2
Fiduciary Duty *13*

A. Understanding Fiduciary Duty *13*

B. Responsible Board Decisions Are Protected *15*

C. The Duty of Care *15*

vii

D. The University Governance Professional Is Your Best Friend   16

E. Never Take Off the Fiduciary Hat   17

CHAPTER 3
Conflict of Interest   18

A. Understanding Conflict of Interest   18

B. Identifying a Conflict   20

C. When to Declare   20

D. An Example of How to Deal with a Conflict of Interest   21

E. An Additional Note: Conflicts and Internal Board Members   22

F. Conclusion   23

PART TWO | BEING PREPARED: UNDERSTANDING THIS UNIQUE SECTOR   25

CHAPTER 4
A Framework for Diligence   27

A. Introduction   27

B. Multi-stakeholder Issues   28

   1) The Board's Role in Positive Cultural Change: Equity, Diversity, and Inclusion   28
   2) Seven Principles of Diversity and Inclusion   29
   3) Technology   31

C. Conclusion   33

CHAPTER 5
Key Internal Stakeholders: Students   34

A. Some Background Information   34

B. Student Engagement Is Important   35

C. Students and Equity, Diversity, and Inclusion   36

D. Social Issues: Key Priorities   37

1) Student Mental Health   37
   2) Accommodation of Students with Disabilities   38
   3) Sexual Violence   38
   4) Racism: Anti-Black Racism in 2020   40
   5) Racism: Indigenous Students   41

E. Other Thoughts About Students   41
   1) Affordability: Tuition and Student Debt   41
   2) Competition for Students   42
   3) Educational Malpractice Claims by Students   42
   4) Alumni   44

F. Conclusion   45

CHAPTER 6
Key Internal Stakeholders: Faculty   46

A. Background Information   46

B. The Work of Faculty   48

C. Systemic Barriers for Women and Racialized Faculty   49

D. Faculty Age Demographics   51

E. Unionization   52

F. Tenure and Promotion   53
   1) Tenure and the Board   54
   2) University Structure and Tenure   56
   3) Part-Time Faculty   57

G. Conclusion   58

CHAPTER 7
Key Internal Stakeholders: Administration   59

A. Organizational Structure and Its Importance to the Board   60

B. Key Roles   60
   1) Chancellor   60
   2) President and Vice-Chancellor   61
   3) Chief Academic Officer   61

4) Chief Research Officer   62
   5) Chief Financial Officer   63
   6) Advancement Executive   63
   7) Governance Professional   64
   8) Legal Counsel   64
   9) Other Functions and Executives   65

CHAPTER 8
Key External Stakeholders: Government   66

A. Key External Stakeholders   66

B. Governments: The Background   66

C. Provincial Governments   67

   1) University Legislation   67
   2) Funding   69
   3) Board Appointees   70

D. Federal Government   72

   1) Operations   72
   2) Research Funding   72
   3) Student Support   73

E. Municipal Government   73

F. Conclusion   74

CHAPTER 9
Key External Stakeholders: Community   75

A. Indigenous Peoples   75

B. Donors   76

C. Partners: Institutions and Industry   78

D. The Community   79

E. Conclusion   80

   Appendix 9.1 | Truth and Reconciliation Commission: Calls to Action   81

CHAPTER 10

Key External Stakeholders: Groups and Associations *82*

A. Types of Groups and Associations *82*

    1) Academic Associations *82*
    2) Faculty Associations *83*
    3) Administrative Associations *83*
    4) Student Associations *84*
    5) Athletic Associations *84*

B. An Introduction to Some National University Associations *85*

    1) Universities Canada *85*
    2) Canadian Association of University Teachers *86*
    3) Canadian Federation of Students and Canadian Alliance of Student Associations *88*

C. Rankings Entities *88*

D. Conclusion *89*

CHAPTER 11

Unique and Essential Concepts *90*

A. All Things "Academic" *90*

B. Universities as a "Commons" *91*

C. Institutional Autonomy *91*

D. Collegiality *94*

E. Governance: Bicameral and Other Models *95*

F. Bicameral Governance and Unionization *96*

G. Academic Freedom *98*

H. How Is Academic Freedom Different from Freedom of Expression (Speech)? *103*

I. When Will Boards Encounter Academic Freedom and Freedom of Expression (Speech)? *104*

J. Conclusion *106*

PART THREE | GOOD GOVERNANCE IN ACTION 107

CHAPTER 12
Understanding Your University's Governance Structure 109

A. Governing Framework: Legislation and Bylaws 109

B. University Policies 111

C. Board Composition 112

D. Effective Management of a Board That Includes Internal Members 115

    1) Other Stakeholder Appointees 117

E. Composition of Academic Governing Bodies 118

F. Promoting Effective Working Relationships with Academic Governing Bodies 119

CHAPTER 13
The Roles of the Board and the Academic Governing Body 120

A. The Role of the University Board: The Bigger Picture 120

B. Key Functions of the University Board 122

C. Board Powers 123

D. The Name of the Academic Governing Body 124

E. The Purview of the Academic Governing Body 125

F. Powers of the Academic Governing Body 126

G. Conclusion 126

    Appendix 13.1 | A Sample of Powers Delegated to Governing Boards in Five Pieces of Legislation 127

    Appendix 13.2 | A Sample of Powers Delegated to Academic Governing Bodies in Five Pieces of Legislation 146

CHAPTER 14
Shared Governance 159

A. The Parameters of Shared Governance 159

B. Challenges Raised by the Issues of Academic Governing Body Effectiveness *161*

C. The Effect of Faculty Unions upon Academic Governing Bodies *162*
   1) Faculty Self-Government and Increased Participation in University Governance *162*
   2) Unionization *164*

D. Increasing Academic Governing Body Effectiveness *166*

E. The Vital Role of the Governance Professional *167*

F. Conclusion *168*

CHAPTER 15
The Board and the President *169*

A. The Challenge of the Presidential Role *170*

B. Laying the Foundation for a New President to Succeed *172*
   1) Understand the University's Culture *172*
   2) Understand University Expectations Related to Presidential Recruitment *172*

C. Supporting the New President After Installation *175*

D. Conclusion *178*

CHAPTER 16
An Overview of University Finances *179*

A. Funding Models *180*

B. The National Picture: Background Information from Statistics Canada *181*

C. University Revenue *182*
   1) Government Funding *182*
   2) Tuition *183*

D. University Expenditures *184*

E. Financial Trends *184*

F. Financial Issues: What Causes Stakeholder Concerns?   *186*
   1) Budgeting Process   *186*
   2) Substantive Budget Concerns   *187*

G. Conclusion   *188*

CHAPTER 17
Wrapping It Up: Some Important Conclusions   *190*

BIBLIOGRAPHY   *195*

INDEX   *209*

ABOUT THE AUTHOR   *211*

Preface

As an immigrant from a working-class family and the first person in my family to go to university, I understand the value of a university education—all aspects of it. It was my father, Brian A Foy, who could not contemplate any path for me other than university, and I thank him for that. I treasured my time as an undergraduate at Queen's University, learning to drink coffee and reading Marx, debating with my classmates, and writing essays on the ferry as I rode for free back and forth between Wolfe Island and Kingston. I struggled, sometimes working three jobs, but all of the time believing in the value of the education and feeling privileged to be there.

What a time of growth and empowerment! I graduated from Queen's first with a political studies degree and then with a law degree, both of which have enabled me to appreciate that universities better our society by teaching us to study ourselves, to question our practices, and to strive to do things better. I believe that universities play a central role in our societies. I believe that in order to continue to play that role well, they must strive for excellence in governance. I believe that boards of universities have a crucial role to play. Hence this book!

As I wrote this book, I thought often about my university secretary colleagues across the country. Some of you are retired, some of you are mid-career, and some of you have just started. We are a dedicated, fun, quirky, and kind group, and I am grateful for the collegiality (meant in the everyday non-academic sense—*ha-ha*—that's university secretary humour) that we show each other daily. I wrote this book to help you as you work with your boards and your leadership teams. Thank you to Sheree Drummond (University of Toronto) and Jeff Leclerc (University of Manitoba) for taking considerable time to review this book and provide truly helpful comments. Thanks also to my former board chair Douglas Allingham for reviewing the book from the perspective of an external governor, and for providing carefully considered and invaluable comments and insight. Thanks to Louis Charpentier (formerly University of Toronto) for your mentorship and support over the years.

This is my first book and I've enjoyed the whole process—the learning, the writing, the editing, the sharing, and the feedback. More work needs to be done in university governance and I hope that this is the start of the dialogue and that I can continue to make contributions to it.

This book was written in the spaces with time stolen from evenings, weekends, and vacations, and I could not have written it without the support and forbearance of my family—my mother, Doris, and my daughter, Annie. I have to include a thanks to my English family, always cheering me on from across the Atlantic. Thank you to Dr Steven Murphy, a university president who understands and is committed to excellence in governance. Thank you to those of my Ontario Tech team members who work directly to support good governance at our institution; most notably, Becky Dinwoodie and Niall O'Halloran. Thanks also to my other team members. You are wonderful colleagues with vision, determination, and dedication, and you make work fun—we continue to complete so much together.

I am grateful.

Cheryl Foy
April 2021
Toronto, Ontario

INTRODUCTION

Welcome to University Governance

> Governance constitutes the medium through which ideas are turned into actions on campus. It is the way things happen and the way they get done. Broadly defined, the concept of "governance" encompasses all of the "structure and processes through which institutional participants interact with and influence each other and communicate with the larger environment."[1]

This book is written for you if you are thinking of joining, or are already a member of, the governing board of one of Canada's more than 150 universities.[2] It is also written to support university governance professionals and will be of interest to members of government, consultants, lawyers, mediators, arbitrators, and others who work closely with universities. This is intended to be a practical rather than theoretical book—interesting and engaging to those in university governance, those for whom the topic is

---

1   Mark G Edelstein, "Academic Governance: The Art of Herding Cats" in James Martin & James E Samels, *First Among Equals: The Role of the Chief Academic Officer* (Baltimore: Johns Hopkins University Press, 1997) at 58.
2   Theresa Shanahan, Michelle Nilson & Li-Jeen Broshko, *Handbook of Canadian Higher Education Law* (Kingston: School of Policy Studies, Queen's University, 2015) at 38. There are 163 provincially "recognized" public and private universities (including theological schools) with degree-granting status authorized by a provincial government.

relatively new, and those who have worked in governance for a while and would like a resource that connects their daily work to patterns in the sector.

Even faculty and staff within universities should find it helpful as, in my experience, looking at universities through a governance lens requires opening your eyes and using a whole new pair of glasses. Although you may work at a university, playing an effective role in university governance involves understanding the decision-making structure and allocation of responsibilities inside your university. Working effectively on a board means setting aside any notions of representing partisan interests and thinking holistically about the university and its best interests. Each university is different and so it is important not to make assumptions.

I have written this book because, having worked with boards for almost twenty years, and within the university context for about half of that, I want to see governance continue to improve at universities. To me, the result of good governance is the removal of barriers—barriers to effective communication, barriers to effective decision-making, barriers to productive, positive, and meaningful change. I believe that good governance makes a difference. I believe that universities are generally not very good at governance for several reasons: (1) university governance takes place within one of the most complex governance environments, (2) universities rightly view themselves as different from the rest of the world but wrongly as above the challenges and issues that have caused the rest of the world to focus on governance as a discipline requiring attention and care, and (3) universities are generally slow to hire and keep governance professionals—those who understand governance and can provide governance leadership and expertise.

It is my hope that over time (because all things within this wonderful sector must be mulled over, chewed, regurgitated, examined, and mulled over again), this book sows the seed of positive governance change within universities. Without sounding dramatic, I believe the future of university autonomy, the bedrock of so many aspects of university culture, depends on it. University boards and academic governing bodies must work together, each within their own spheres, and in a complementary way, to advance the mission of their institutions. In short, if we can't make collegial governance work, the alternative will not be faculty self-governance. Given the way the pendulum is swinging, the most likely alternative is increased government control, an outcome that I would argue is in no stakeholder's interest.

This book introduces you to the aspects of governance that are unique to universities. It's a book intended to help you learn about the sector so that you can contribute more fully and feel more engaged. New university board members, even internal board members (students, staff, faculty, or other members of the university community who are permitted to serve on the university board) often lose confidence when they realize how much there is to learn. New members quickly begin to realize that the scope of issues faced by universities, the complex relationship between universities and key stakeholders, and the increasing role of governments in university governance make the university board experience daunting, challenging, and incredibly exciting. For internal members it may be challenging to shift gears from the more focused perspective you typically have to the broad perspective you need. The unique concepts and context of university governance may lead new board members to sit back and "go along to get along" because they lack the confidence to engage early, effectively, and often. But that isn't your role. You are a fiduciary from the date of your appointment until your term is finished, and so there's no sitting back! Let's go!

— Part One —

Joining a University Board? Understanding the Commitment You Are Making

CHAPTER 1

What to Consider

A. WHY SHOULD YOU JOIN A UNIVERSITY BOARD?

When joining a university board, you become part of the rich and enduring history of higher education, as "[m]ost of the Western institutions in existence five hundred years ago that survive today are universities."[1] For those who are interested in becoming a member of a governing board, university boards are attractive. Although roles are generally unpaid, university boards have a high public profile, offer a chance to serve the community, provide opportunities to learn from and engage with a network of individuals from many other sectors, and provide excellent, if challenging, governance training for those board members hoping to later seek a role on a paid board. Universities are sizeable institutions with strong roots and traditions.

Universities are exciting places that "have become one of the most important institutions in our society."[2] They are at the forefront of research and teaching and are engaged in some pretty amazing developments. It is inspiring to be a part of institutions that "exist to develop the human intellect, to enable discernment and the search for truth, and to resist ignorance,

---

1   Peter MacKinnon, *University Commons Divided: Exploring Debate and Dissent on Campus* (Toronto: University of Toronto Press, 2018) at 90.
2   Ian Austin & Glen A Jones, *Governance of Higher Education: Global Perspectives, Theories and Practices* (New York: Routledge, 2015) at 1.

intellectual laziness and coercion."[3] They play an important role in our society. They are expected to be drivers of, guides to, and facilitators of social change. They are the places where we can have honest and protected conversations about the things happening in our societies. As corporate entities, they have a large number of stakeholders. As educators and recipients of significant public funds, they are the focus of public opinion, of close financial scrutiny, and they must work within continuously changing government policy and increasing regulation.

If you want to make a meaningful contribution to an institution with an important mission and get great governance experience at the same time, you've picked the right place. In the wake of the COVID-19 pandemic in 2020, universities will need good governance more than ever. As Alex Usher notes, "The system will survive, but it is not yet guaranteed that all individual institutions will do so in their current form."[4] I encourage you to take the leap and get involved with university governance.

B. UNIVERSITIES ARE COMPLEX PLACES TO GOVERN

While university board roles offer a tremendous opportunity to board members, universities are important and complex organizations, so serving on a board should not be undertaken lightly. To illustrate the point (without scaring you off!):

> Universities are not simple organizations. In fact, given the breadth of their goals and missions, the tremendous expertise and specialization that characterize their basic functions, and the huge diversity of their activities, universities have evolved to become one of the most complex organization forms that the human species have ever created. They employ hundreds, and in some cases thousands, of highly specialized experts who share their knowledge through teaching and pursue what are frequently unique programs of research. The university's physical plant includes classrooms and laboratories, but it also may include medical centers, restaurants, rental housing, museums, art galleries, spaces for worship, and a plethora of specialized research facilities, ranging from agriculture research lands, to supercomputing facilities to nuclear reactors.[5]

---

3   MacKinnon, above note 1 at 90.
4   Alex Usher, "The State of Postsecondary Education in Canada, 2020" (Toronto: Higher Education Strategy Associates) at 11.
5   Austin & Jones, above note 2 at 1.

A former university board chair, Douglas Allingham, advises that university boards are "not starter boards" and those wishing to serve on a university board should have prior board experience.[6] Given the history, culture, size, and complexity of universities, the governance environment is unique. One of the drivers of this book was to share knowledge about that unique environment. If you come to the board with governance training or experience, it will serve you well. However, you need to come knowing that you have a lot to learn, because the university governance context is very different. Serving on a university board demands commitment and time. It takes time just to understand the organization of the institution and the types of activities in which it is engaged.

As well, the compliance environment within which universities operate is highly complex. As Peter MacKinnon notes:

> If we explore the A-Z directory on any Canadian university website, we glimpse the modern and regulated university world: animal care, disability services, discrimination, harassment, investment research protocols and ethics, risk management, insurance, safety, and sustainability — the list goes on.[7]

Understanding the university's commitments in these areas is exacting. In addition to the governance challenge, the expectation that board members will support the fundraising efforts of the university by opening doors and making introductions, and by making personal donations, is growing. Undertaking university board governance is a weighty responsibility.

C. EDUCATE YOURSELF ABOUT THE UNIVERSITY AND YOUR ROLE

It's important that prospective board members understand that board members are in place to oversee significant corporate entities with substantial assets and responsibilities. Before engaging you as a board member, the university will want an assurance of your ability to make the required time commitment and this is something to consider seriously. The role you are about to undertake is an important one, and if you don't have time to read and digest the materials and fully prepare so that you are an engaged board member, you should not apply. In order to understand the commitment

---

6   From a conversation with the author.
7   MacKinnon, above note 1 at 90.

you are making, you should carefully review the university's website to gain an understanding of the university.

Attached as Appendix 1.1 to this chapter is a list of questions you might want to ask prior to applying for a role on the board. Look at the profiles of other board members and speak with one or more of them. Research the university's leadership. Look at the mission, vision, values, and any strategic plans. Board meetings usually have a public component and minutes of the public meetings should be available on the university's website under "governance." Minutes will give you a sense of the work the board has recently undertaken. Begin as you mean to go on — be prepared for your interview and for the work of a university board member. There is a lot resting on it.

APPENDIX 1.1

Questions to ask to understand what is expected of a university board member:

1) What is the board meeting schedule?
2) Is there an annual retreat?
3) Am I expected to sit on one or more committees?
4) What is the committee schedule?
5) What are the board attendance policies?
    i. Can I attend electronically?
    ii. How many meetings am I expected to attend in person?
6) Are the board members expected to attend other university events?
    i. Convocation?
    ii. Fundraising events?
    iii. Faculty and educational events?
    iv. Community events?
    v. Student and sports events?
    vi. Other?
7) Does the university offer and expect board members to attend orientation, professional development, and other training sessions (and what are the expectations related to training)?
8) Are there expectations for board members to play a leadership role within the board (committee chairs, board vice-chairs, board chair)?
    i. How many leadership roles are there on the board?
    ii. How are the leadership roles selected?
9) Does the university use a skills matrix as a recruitment tool? If yes:
    i. What perspective do you anticipate I will bring?
    ii. What skills from your skills matrix are you looking to me to contribute?
10) What expectations does the university have about my involvement in fundraising?
11) What are the significant and relevant board policies such as the code of conduct, and where can they be found?
12) How are board members protected from liability (indemnification provisions in bylaws and liability insurance coverage)?
13) Does the board have any major projects coming up?
14) When is the president's term up for renewal? (Note: presidential recruitment is the board's responsibility and the recruitment process within a university is extensive and consultative. It takes a lot of time.)

15) What is the board's culture?
    i. Are there divisions on the board?
    ii. What is being done to improve board culture?
16) How do board practices support board member development? Does the board assign mentors?
17) How does the board assess current levels of engagement by board members and how does the board promote board member engagement?
18) What is the institution's strategy, and how does the board support strategic planning?
19) How does the board maintain a strategic focus?
20) What is the balance between strategic work and the oversight responsibilities of the board?

CHAPTER 2

Fiduciary Duty

If you've held a leadership role or engaged in any board training at all, you will understand that board members have two primary legal duties: (1) a fiduciary duty, and (2) a duty of care.

A. UNDERSTANDING FIDUCIARY DUTY

Fiduciary duty is a duty of loyalty to the corporate entity. It's a duty that arises in Canadian corporate legislation and likely makes an appearance either explicitly or implicitly in your university's governing legislation, bylaws, and policies. A fiduciary holds the highest trust obligation at law. When I was in law school, one of my professors asked my class to think of the corporate entity as a vulnerable little baby. Bear with me as I explain! The fiduciaries are those board members and senior leaders entrusted with the care of the baby, acting in the interests of the baby, serving the baby with honesty and good faith, putting the baby's interests before their own, and pledging loyalty. The baby analogy illustrates the degree of vulnerability of a corporate entity that must act through the humans entrusted with its care and leadership.

Lawyers who offer training on fiduciary duty will often explain the concept by reference to cases. A favourite is *BCE v 1976 Debentureholders*. This case is so often referenced because it is an important case in which the

Supreme Court of Canada made a few things clear about the director's duty to the corporate entity.

1) Directors have a duty to act in the best interests of the corporate entity.
2) Acting in the best interests of the corporate entity involves ensuring that individual stakeholders are treated "fairly and equitably."[1]
3) Directors have a duty to consider each decision on its own merits considering "all the circumstances" and "all relevant considerations."[2]
4) There are no hard and fast rules about one set of interests taking precedence over another set of interests and "everything depends on the situation."[3]
5) It's also true that the interests of stakeholders will be different and directors will prioritize the interests of some stakeholders over those of others in certain situations. Sometimes directors will make decisions that will make some stakeholders unhappy.

It would be understandable if your response to the court's decision is a sarcastic "Oh, great!" I understand that an "it depends on the situation, you make the call" type of answer might be seen as a little unhelpful. But worry not, because this book is going to help you apply the concept of fiduciary duty. There's a further piece of good news on this point. We also have some clarity about what behaviour is consistent with fiduciary obligations:

- **Confidentiality**: Treat all information you receive as confidential unless it's very clear to you that it's not confidential. Understand the nature of your confidentiality obligations and understand that some obligations endure indefinitely (such as any information or documents pertaining to presidential search committee deliberations), while other obligations may be limited to a defined period (such as confidential information in a contractual agreement). When in any doubt, keep information you believe to be confidential, confidential.
- **Conflict of Interest**: Avoid conflicts of interest and promptly disclose one you have. Never vote on a matter that involves you in a conflict of interest. Because conflict of interest is poorly understood, I've included a separate chapter on that. See Chapter 3.

---

1   *BCE Inc v 1976 Debentureholders*, 2008 SCC 69 at para 66 [*BCE*].
2   *Ibid* at para 82.
3   *Ibid* at para 84.

- **True Purpose**: All activity that you pursue as a board member should be pursued with a true purpose that arises only out of the university's best interests.
- **No Pursuit of University Opportunities or Use of University Confidential Information**: Ensure that you do not take advantage of university information or opportunities for your own benefit.

B. RESPONSIBLE BOARD DECISIONS ARE PROTECTED

Another proposition that the *BCE* case stands for is that responsible board decisions are protected.[4] The court affirmed what is commonly known as the "business judgment" rule. The business judgment rule provides that decisions of directors about which interests to consider and how to balance those interests will be respected (and most importantly won't attract liability) if the decisions are made responsibly. A key part of this book is focused on tips for demonstrating appropriate consideration of interests and stakeholders so that you and your board can make good decisions and can demonstrate responsible decision-making.

> **Best Practice Tip:** It is important that board decisions are recorded in such a way that it is clear that the board fulfilled its fiduciary obligations in making the decision. Your governance professional must fully understand the business judgment rule and fiduciary obligations so that, particularly for important decisions, minutes are drafted to demonstrate and support the process followed by the board in reaching the decision. Note that your governance professional is often focused on this and can provide really good advice about what process to follow to ensure that the board can demonstrate that it has followed defensible decision-making processes.

C. THE DUTY OF CARE

Your fiduciary obligations also involve what is known as a "duty of care." This duty involves each board member exercising the care, diligence, and skill that a reasonably prudent person would exercise in comparable circumstances. By making the reference point the "reasonably prudent person," the standard becomes an objective one, which means board member

---

4   *Ibid.*

behaviour is measured not by what the board member thinks is right, nor even by what the board as a whole thinks, but rather by what is judged that an independent and reasonably prudent person would likely do in the circumstances.

It's important to note that board members have a duty to employ the skill and knowledge they possess. When advised of this, lawyers, accountants, and other professionals may feel that they are unfairly held to a higher standard. It is true that the more skill and knowledge a board member has, the higher the standard to which the member may be held. For example, a board member who is a compensation consultant will be held to a higher standard in respect of decisions relating to the university's pension, benefits, and compensation plans.

The duty of care involves each individual member being able to demonstrate diligence in its role. Diligence is demonstrated in many ways. In a nutshell, you'll go a long way to demonstrating diligence if you

1) attend meetings;
2) educate yourself through participation in professional development opportunities and engage with the university community;
3) prepare for the meetings by reading your materials in advance;
4) ask good questions and always consider alternatives to the options being proposed;
5) demonstrate that you are acting in the best interests of the university by raising issues and asking questions that show you are thinking about the impact of decisions on key stakeholders;
6) rely on the governance expertise of your governance professional, and;
7) recognize when it makes sense to rely on external expertise and engage experts as appropriate to advise the board.

D. THE UNIVERSITY GOVERNANCE PROFESSIONAL IS YOUR BEST FRIEND

Those supporting the board and sometimes the academic governing body inside universities are typically called "university secretary," a title akin to the "corporate secretary" with which many may be more familiar. The nature of the governance professional's role is difficult and complex because the politics of university governance can be incredibly challenging. It is important for the board and the president to support the governance professional who is the keeper of good governance at the institution.

The university governance professional helps the president and the senior leadership team engage with the board at the right level, effectively and efficiently, and with integrity. The person in this role manages the workflow for the board and ensures that board requests are tracked and fulfilled. This role champions governance and supports the board to work at the strategic and oversight level, avoiding the operational weeds. This role identifies board engagement issues and professional development opportunities by assisting the board chair to see patterns of behaviour or gaps in knowledge. The person who occupies the university secretary role and does it well is crucial to good university governance.

E. NEVER TAKE OFF THE FIDUCIARY HAT

I love using hats to help think about fiduciary duty. It really helps to be mindful about the hats you are wearing when you sit at the board table. To protect yourself and the institution, and to be a good board member and support effective board decision-making, always wear your fiduciary hat. It should never come off. If worn correctly, your hat will help you consistently identify the pressures and uncertainties that may interfere with you asserting yourself, expressing your views, and asking good questions. You have a job to do. As one of my former board chairs used to say, "Don't just show up for the hot lunch!"

CHAPTER 3

Conflict of Interest

A. UNDERSTANDING CONFLICT OF INTEREST

This concept is poorly understood, and sometimes people's self-interest is such that it affects their ability to see that they are in a conflict. Most universities have a conflict-of-interest policy and procedure. You should make it a priority to be familiar with these documents. A conflict of interest is simply something that affects your ability to objectively make a decision that considers only the best interests of the university because you may derive a personal benefit from that decision. I think of conflicts of interest as things that cloud our judgment and get in the way of our ability to put the university first. Making a decision while in a conflict of interest may result in a poor outcome for the university, and will most certainly affect perceptions of your integrity as a board member. However, remember that you are on a board to make decisions. It is one of your key responsibilities. As such, be sure to understand conflicts of interest and do not declare one lightly.

University boards are sometimes described as "stakeholder boards" because every university board includes board members selected from stakeholder groups such as faculty, staff, students, and alumni, among others. This stakeholder composition is one of the unique elements of university governance discussed in more detail in Chapter 12. The inclusion of internal members on the university board makes it yet more important to understand conflicts of interest and have a robust and consistently applied process for managing them. Rather than making things awkward, having a regular and open practice of declaring conflicts of interest builds trust around the board table and it's a good way for internal members to demonstrate credibility.

As you improve your understanding of conflicts of interest and encounter them in board work, keep in mind the ideas below.

- **There's nothing wrong with *being* in a conflict of interest.** Board members often feel that they have done something wrong if they are in a conflict of interest. This is not true. Conflicts of interest happen without individuals having done anything wrong. It's what you do about the conflict of interest that matters. (Hint: disclose it!)
- **It doesn't matter if you think you can be objective.** This is where you can go wrong. Board members often think that they are capable of being objective even if they have a financial or personal interest in the outcome. That may or may not be true but it's not the point. For your own protection and for the protection of the integrity of the board's decision-making process, if you are in a conflict, withdraw from decision-making. You are protecting the integrity of the board's decision by ensuring that no one can undermine or attack the decision on the basis that one of the board members involved in the decision appears to have conflicting interests.
- **It's failing to remove yourself from decision-making when you are in a conflict that is the "wrong."** You can only go wrong if you fail to recognize it, fail to declare it, and fail to take yourself out of any decision-making process associated with the conflict of interest situation.
- **Avoiding a conflict of interest is a board member's personal obligation.** It's your duty, and no one else's, to identify and declare conflicts and act accordingly. If you make a decision by voting on a motion while in a conflict of interest you may attract liability, and lose the trust of your fellow board members. You may also undermine the confidence of the board's stakeholders in the decision and indeed their willingness to abide by or respect the decision. Your behaviour should be beyond reproach—always.
- **Should you stay for the discussion?** Once a conflict is declared, it means that everyone else is aware that there exists an interest that might affect your judgment. The better practice is to leave the room while the matter with which you have a conflict is discussed because

your presence may have a chilling effect on discussion. My perspective is that there are situations where it may be in the university's interests to hear the views of the person with the conflict, and as long as policy or procedure permits it, the board may also allow this person to express an opinion.

B. IDENTIFYING A CONFLICT

Conflicts of interest fall into two main categories:

1) **Financial:** If you or a family member stand to benefit financially from a decision, you are in a financial conflict of interest.
2) **Personal:** If you or a family member stands to benefit in another way (professional or career advantage, for example) your ability to make a decision only in the best interests of the university is compromised.

> **Best Practice Tip:** Your board should have two processes to facilitate and normalize conflict of interest declarations: (1) an annual declaration process, and (2) a process for declaring and handling conflict of interest at each meeting.

C. WHEN TO DECLARE

Annually: Your board should have a process whereby it canvasses annually for known conflicts of interest. This allows the board governance professional to track these and include them in the chair's notes as matters come forward. Be sure to declare potentially repetitive conflicts through the board's annual process. If there is no annual process, you should write to the board chair annually, copying the governance professional, confirming your potentially conflicting interests. For example, I am aware of a situation in which an accounting professional provided services to one of the unions on campus. That person made sure that the board was aware of the relationship with the union and diligently asked the university secretary each time an issue that could cause a conflict came up, so that he could know whether or not to declare a conflict at a particular meeting. This is the kind of diligence that is required.

At the Meeting: Even if there is an annual declaration, if a board member has a conflict of interest in respect of a specific item on a board meeting agenda, the board member must declare that conflict of interest. It is best to do this in advance to the chair, copying the governance professional. At the meeting, make sure the declaration is recorded in the meeting minutes.

D. AN EXAMPLE OF HOW TO DEAL WITH A CONFLICT OF INTEREST

University board member Celia is a very senior employee of a municipal government. The university has the following types of regular dealings with the municipal government:

1) Building permits and construction matters
2) Security and policing
3) Town–gown issues related to student activity and student conduct
4) Municipal government has been a donor
5) Joint lobbying of provincial and federal government for funding and support of local development
6) Municipal transportation

At its next meeting, the university will be considering a decision to enter into an agreement with the municipality relating to a universal transit pass for students. Under this agreement, the municipality will agree to allow students carrying a university pass to use the transit system for a price that is much lower than single ticket fares.

Now, let's look at the conflict declaration obligations in this example.

General: Given all of the points of common interest between the university and the municipality, you can see that Celia would have obligations to further the interests of the municipality in all of these areas, and there would be many examples of regular conflicts. In this situation, confirming with the university annually the potential for conflict is a good practice.

You might note that the university probably already knows where this board member works. **That's true but misses the point:** This is the board member demonstrating the board member's awareness of the conflict and the obligations related to the conflict.

Specific: Celia would also make a specific conflict of interest declaration at the meeting to decide the transit agreement. The board member could, with the board's leave, express a view about the topic, but should not participate in voting.

Should the person in conflict leave the room? There's often a question about whether a person in conflict should leave the room. Sometimes boards are embarrassed to ask a person to leave. Here is a benefit of having a clear university policy or procedure and following it. However, where the path is not prescribed by policy or procedure, the board professional and board chair should give thought to this issue in advance of the meeting.

The person in conflict should leave the room if the board chair assesses that remaining could have a chilling effect on the voting choices of the board. Let's say that two other board members work with companies that regularly deal with the municipality (engineering or construction companies, for example). If Celia remains in the room during the vote, these two board members may feel pressure to vote the way they think the municipality would want them to vote. The board chair, in consultation with the board professional, should carefully assess this, and it's usually best if the board member in conflict is advised ahead of time of the requirement to leave the room. The easiest way to deal with such issues of influence, of course, is to have the member in conflict always leave the room, but in the absence of policy or procedure, that's a judgment call for the board. Whatever decision is made, the approach should be consistent, and preserving the integrity of board decision-making processes should be paramount.

E. AN ADDITIONAL NOTE: CONFLICTS AND INTERNAL BOARD MEMBERS

It is worthwhile to note that there may be situations in which internal board members are permitted to discuss and vote on matters in which they have a personal interest. Students, for example, may be permitted by practice or by policy, bylaw, or legislation to participate in discussing and voting on tuition and fees if the fees apply generally to the whole student body and not to that student individually. The same may apply to faculty and employee board members in respect of salary and benefits changes. For example, the *University of Ontario Institute of Technology Act, 2002* provides exceptions for employee and student conflicts:

> (6) Despite subsection (4), a member of the board who is also an employee of the university may take part in discussing and voting on issues concerning general conditions of employment for university employees, unless the discussion and voting deals with the circumstances

of the particular employee as an isolated issue, separate and apart from consideration of other employees.

(7) Despite subsection (4), a member of the board who is also a student may take part in discussing and voting on issues concerning students generally, unless such discussion and voting deals with the circumstances of the particular student as an isolated issue, separate and apart from consideration of other students.[1]

Brock University achieves the same result by way of policy. In its *Board of Trustees Conflict of Interest Policy*, Brock University describes these acceptable conflicts as "structural conflicts"[2] and provides that faculty, staff, and students are not considered to have a conflict when they are part of a group and "where their interest is the same or substantially the same as any other faculty, staff or student member of the University."[3] Note, however, that this policy goes on to prohibit employees from voting on "matters related to the remuneration or benefits, pension, terms of employment, rights or privileges available to employees of the University that are directly related to compensation or that are negotiated in a collective fashion for a class or group of employees of the University."[4]

Both internal and external board members should be sure to understand the particular conflict of interest rules applicable to them.

F. CONCLUSION

As board members, your obligations are to understand when you are in a conflict, declare the conflict, and remove yourself from decisions in which you have a conflict. As a board, creating a culture in which conflict-of-interest processes are normalized and are a regular part of board process is crucial. Take steps to ensure your boards understand conflict of interest and create a culture in which being transparent and thoughtful about conflicts of interest are encouraged.

---

1   *University of Ontario Institute of Technology Act, 2002*, SO 2002, c 8, Sched O, s 9(6) & (7), online: www.ontario.ca/laws/statute/02u08.
2   *Board of Trustees Conflict of Interest Policy* (Brock University, 26 September 2019), point 4, online: www.brocku.ca/university-secretariat/wp-content/uploads/sites/82/2019-09-26-Board-COI-Policy.pdf.
3   *Ibid*, point 4.
4   *Ibid*, point 5.

– *Part Two* –

Being Prepared: Understanding This Unique Sector

CHAPTER 4

A Framework for Diligence

A. INTRODUCTION

In Chapter 2, I advised that one of the ways in which a board member can demonstrate diligence is by raising issues and asking questions that show that the board member is thinking about the effect of decisions on key stakeholders, as well as on the university as a whole. By doing this, the board member is using a stakeholder framework to approach decisions. Board members should keep a (mental or written) list of stakeholders. Each time the board makes a decision, the board members should be considering and asking about the effect of that decision on one or more stakeholders. In doing so, board members will be demonstrating diligence. At the same time, the informed and probing questions that the board members are asking should improve the decisions the board makes.

Board members must remember that the stakeholders affected by each decision will change. Each new decision means identifying the affected stakeholders anew. The relative impact of a decision on stakeholder groups will also change and so in one decision a board might prioritize the interests of students and in another the interests of a key partner. Therefore, the second step in developing the framework is to order the stakeholders according to impact. Finally, board members should step back and consider that issue's impact across the university and collectively on all stakeholders. For example, as the board considers initiatives to combat racism in the university community, it must consider how racism affects the student experience. A different analysis and different information will inform the board's consideration of racism against faculty and staff. A further analysis is required when considering racism in the context of the university community's role within the broader community.

Chapters 5 through 10 introduce you to key university stakeholders, their roles, and the interests and issues that affect them. As you get to know your university better, you may identify other stakeholders. Your knowledge of your stakeholders and their interests will enable you as a board member to demonstrate diligence, to better consider the interests of university stakeholders as individual groups, and collectively, and to make better decisions.

B. MULTI-STAKEHOLDER ISSUES

There are issues that affect multiple stakeholders, and before describing key university stakeholders, it's worthwhile to provide a description of these multi-stakeholder issues, as boards will undoubtedly encounter them.

1) The Board's Role in Positive Cultural Change: Equity, Diversity, and Inclusion

Issues of equity, diversity, and inclusion thread their way through the discussions of multiple stakeholders below, particularly in the discussions of students and faculty. Many issues fall within the broad topic of university culture. Boards are ultimately responsible for university culture and for creating a culture in which impediments to inclusion are abolished. Boards should ask and ensure they have the answers to three key questions:

1) How is the board fostering inclusion within the board?
2) How is the board ensuring a culture of inclusion across the university?
3) How is the university fulfilling its role as a leader in positive social change?

These questions aren't to be asked and answered only once. Cultural change is effected and then maintained over time. The job of asking questions never ends, and the board should dedicate time to understanding indicators of university culture and dedicate time to understanding university culture and prioritizing changes to be implemented.

No university is immune from hate, violence, and discrimination against equity-seeking groups, and vigilance is required. It behooves board members to understand the framework of diversity and inclusion within which universities strive to operate. A word of caution to you as individuals — your individual and personal opinions about issues of equity, diversity, and inclusion are not to supplant information received from university stakeholders themselves. Well-prepared board members understand their own biases and prejudices and work hard to put them aside; it's another way of ensuring decisions are made in the best interests of the university. Unless you are an expert in a particular area, you are best advised to rely on data and the expertise of others. As a university board member, you are not making decisions for yourself. Your role is to support the building of an inclusive institution at which people from all backgrounds are safe to study.

2) Seven Principles of Diversity and Inclusion

Between the time I began writing this book and the time it was finished, tragic events, including the murder of George Floyd in May 2020, had given new life to discussions about racism. There were many initiatives already in place to tackle racism at universities, and there are more in development as a result of these events. In 2017, university leaders from across the country committed to seven principles of diversity and inclusion.[1]

1. We believe our universities are enriched by diversity and inclusion. As leaders of universities that aspire to be diverse, fair and open, we will make our personal commitment to diversity and inclusion evident.
2. We commit our institutions to developing and/or maintaining an equity, diversity and inclusion action plan in consultation with students, faculty, staff and administrators, and particularly with individuals from under-represented groups. We commit to demonstrating progress over time.
3. We commit to taking action to provide equity of access and opportunity. To do so, we will identify and address barriers to, and provide supports for, the recruitment and retention of senior university leaders, university Board and Senate members, faculty, staff and students, particularly from under-represented groups.

---

1   For example, the work of Dr Wisdom Tettey & Karima Hashmani at the University of Toronto to promote a national university dialogue on anti-Black racism, "Canadian Universities and Colleges Come Together to Take Action on Anti-Black Racism," *U of T News* (16 July 2020), online: www.utoronto.ca/news/u-t-led-national-dialogue-address-anti-black-racism-higher-education.

4. We will work with our faculty and staff, search firms, and our governing boards to ensure that candidates from all backgrounds are provided support in their career progress and success in senior leadership positions at our institutions.
5. We will seek ways to integrate inclusive excellence throughout our university's teaching, research, community engagement and governance. In doing so, we will engage with students, faculty, staff, our boards of governors, senates and alumni to raise awareness and encourage all efforts.
6. We will be guided in our efforts by evidence, including evidence of what works in addressing any barriers and obstacles that may discourage members of under-represented groups to advance. We commit to sharing evidence of practices that are working, in Canada and abroad, with higher education institutions.
7. Through our national membership organization, Universities Canada, we will work to generate greater awareness of the importance of diversity and inclusive excellence throughout Canadian higher education.[2]

The board should work to understand key concepts such as "intersectionality." I recommend a TED talk by Kimberlé Crenshaw, the woman who coined the term "intersectionality" to describe how injustice and inequity are increased for people who are from multiple equity-seeking groups.[3] In her video, Ms Crenshaw uses the audience to demonstrate that people are aware of the names of Black men killed by police, but are not aware of the names of Black women killed by police, making the point that Black women are discriminated against because of both race and gender. The board's role is to oversee the efforts to combat racism on campus, to ensure there are plans in place, and to ensure that they are monitored such that they achieve real progress. The board should remain cognizant of the important leadership role that universities play with respect to assisting Canadian society to understand and address societal issues such as systemic racism, sexism, and sexual violence.

---

[2] "Universities Canada Principles on Equity, Diversity, and Inclusion," Universities Canada (26 October 2017), online: Universities Canada www.univcan.ca/media-room/media-releases/universities-canada-principles-equity-diversity-inclusion.

[3] See online: www.ted.com/talks/kimberle_crenshaw_the_urgency_of_intersectionality?language=en#t-299404.

3) Technology

Technology is another multi-stakeholder issue. Technology is changing how students want to learn, the methods available for teaching, and the locations from which students can learn and faculty can teach. It is changing the way that faculty and students work together. While the COVID-19 pandemic has accelerated the use of technology in the virtual classroom, this change was already well underway. The board's role is to understand all of the ways in which technology affects the university. Again, a stakeholder framework can help:

- What do students expect?
- How do faculty want to use technology?
- How does the university see technology as a strategic advantage?
- How can technology be used to create operational efficiencies and how does that affect employees?
- What are the risks and challenges with technology?
- How is privacy affected and how are privacy rights protected?
- How secure is the university infrastructure?
- How is information used?
- What policies need to be in place to govern the way university technology is used?
- How does the university keep up as technology advances?

Students entering university expect to see technology from start to finish — from the application process to graduation, and in all of the steps in between. They expect technology-based way-finding. They expect to be able to reach the administration and faculty electronically. They expect universities to provide an environment in which all of their many devices can access the university information technology systems. They expect to see technology in the classroom. What about people who are less technology savvy coming back to the university? How are they accommodated or supported to manage in a tech world?

Technology changes the way teaching can occur. Faculty can teach from afar. Faculty can use technology in the classroom — everything from YouTube videos to interactive real-time quizzes or real-time polling. Faculty expect high-quality technological research infrastructure. How do faculty and the university stay abreast of technological advances so that courses remain relevant? What technological knowledge and skills do students need to be successful in the workplace?

Universities themselves play an important role in our society. They play an important role in innovation and creation of new technology and in knowledge sharing. What is the university's role in critically examining technological advances? As Dr Steven Murphy notes:

> Today, we have a collective responsibility to explore and research the implications of tech, both positive and negative. That means asking the hard questions: What are the ethical implications of tech? How will it compromise our privacy? How do we address hate bias and extremism on the Web and in social media? What are the biases built into AI [artificial intelligence]?[4]

The university's involvement with technology is thus not limited to the faculties that study or teach technology, such as the faculties of science and engineering. The moral and ethical issues raised by the development of technology and by the pervasive influence of big tech companies on campus must be dealt with by governing bodies.

In March 2019, Macy Bayern provided a summary of the top ten technologies that would affect higher education in the year to come.

1) Next generation security and risk management: Universities are facing daily cyberattacks and must invest in technology to protect their infrastructure and data.
2) AI conversational interfaces: AI can be used to better understand what users want and improve user satisfaction.
3) Smart campus: A smart campus uses electronic hardware and software to provide services like teaching, administration, and utility management through personal electronic devices.
4) Predictive analytics: Predictive analytics uses statistical modelling and data mining to develop algorithms that predict student behaviour. Those predictions can be used to anticipate student demand for university supports and services. For example, by using early indicators of student performance, universities can anticipate the learning support students will need.
5) Nudge tech: Nudge tech is the use of technology to effect positive changes in student behaviour.
6) Digital credentialing tech: Digital credentials can help to protect information and avoid fraud.

---

4 Steven Murphy, "Tech with a Social Conscience: Why You Should Care," *Globe and Mail* (17 April 2019), online: www.theglobeandmail.com/business/careers/leadership/article-tech-with-a-social-conscience-why-you-should-care/.

7) Hybrid integration platforms: Hybrid integration platforms connect data and software applications stored on remote servers. For a university, they can integrate learning management systems (LMS) (used as a primary tool for teachers and students to communicate and share course information) and customer relationship management (CRM) (used by universities to manage recruitment and registration).
8) Career-planning software: Software can track students' progress, skills, and experiences to develop career goals.
9) Student cross-life cycle CRM: CRM supports students while they are at the university and beyond.
10) Wireless presentation technologies.[5]

This list gives you a sense of the ways in which technology is affecting universities. It's happening now, and your board needs to ensure that your university has plans in place to manage it. If universities don't embrace technology, they'll be left behind. As a board member, your role is to ensure that there is a strategy to address technology in university infrastructure, administration, and in the curriculum. The board also has a role in ensuring effective risk management and management of all of the compliance obligations that come with technology.

C. CONCLUSION

It can be difficult for board members to understand how to apply legal concepts such as duty of care and fiduciary duty. This chapter provides an overview of how these concepts can be applied through a stakeholder framework. This involves identifying key stakeholders and the issues affecting them. While the stakeholders identified in this book are common to most universities, each university will have others, and the relative priority of the stakeholders will change. The board's task is to understand its own university, its stakeholders, and their interests. This chapter identifies a number of multi-stakeholder issues. Again, those issues listed are those that appear to be current priorities for most universities. It is the role of each board to ensure it understands the multi-stakeholder issues for their university. Don't worry if it takes time to develop a discipline around this approach to decision making.

---

5   Macy Bayern, "10 Technologies That Will Impact Higher Education the Most This Year," *TechRepublic* (29 March 2019), CBS Interactive online: www.techrepublic.com/article/10-technologies-that-will-impact-higher-education-the-most-this-year.

CHAPTER 5

Key Internal Stakeholders: Students

A. SOME BACKGROUND INFORMATION

Students are a key university stakeholder and it is important to understand them. In 2019, there were approximately 1.4 million full- and part-time students in the Canadian university system.[1] Chapter 16 addresses university finances, but it's safe to say for all universities that students contribute a significant portion of university income, and since 2008 "government income has stagnated while income from students has steadily increased, mainly due to increases in international student numbers."[2]

Although described as one stakeholder, the student body is not homogeneous, of course. This one stakeholder is made up of many groups. The university structure itself divides students by level (undergraduate, graduate, postgraduate), by faculty, and by program of study within a faculty. The student body is also made up of many racial, social, religious, ethnic, socio-economic, and other groups.

Students are changing. Generation X has different characteristics than Generation Y or millennials. Next are Generation Z and Generation Alpha.

---

1 "Facts and Stats," Universities Canada (31 July 2018), online: Universities Canada www.univcan.ca/universities/facts-and-stats.
2 Alex Usher, *The State of Postsecondary Education in Canada, 2020* (Toronto: Higher Education Strategy Associates, 2020) at 31.

It is essential to strategic planning for boards to understand the characteristics and interests of students and subgroups of students. These interests and characteristics drive students' choices of programs of study and also shape their university experiences. For example, Generation Z considers itself more accepting and open-minded than any generation before it. Almost half of Generation Zs are minorities (only 22 percent of baby boomers were minorities), and the majority of Generation Z supports social movements such as Black Lives Matter, transgender rights, and feminism.[3] Of students, Peter MacKinnon writes:

> There are more of them and they are more diverse. They have been courted by the universities they attend, not simply admitted to them. They are consumers and their education is a consumable for which they are attentive to price and satisfaction. They seek engagement, active learning, and a collaborative learning environment, not professor-centred instruction. And their interactions — amongst themselves and with others — are mediated by technology.[4]

There is much to parse in the MacKinnon quotation and we'll look at elements of the quotation a little closer because, as board members, these are things you should be considering.

B. STUDENT ENGAGEMENT IS IMPORTANT

Research shows that student engagement is crucial to student success:

> Decades of research studies on [university] student learning and development point to an unequivocal conclusion: The more time and energy students devote to educationally purposeful activities — studying, interacting with faculty members and peers about substantive matters, practicing and applying what they are learning — the more they typically benefit in terms of a wide range of desired outcomes of college. Those include subject matter knowledge, analytical reasoning, effective writing and speaking, and so on. The observation that effort is key to strong

---

3 "Generation Z News: Latest Characteristics, Research, and Facts," *Business Insider* (n.d.), online: www.businessinsider.com/generation-z.

4 Peter MacKinnon, *University Commons Divided: Exploring Debate and Dissent on Campus* (Toronto: University of Toronto Press, 2018) at 3–4.

performance holds for every field of endeavor and setting and explains why student engagement is integral to student learning.[5]

Your board should understand the engagement level of your university students. Luckily, there is information available to you! Many universities (in fact, more than 1,600 institutions in North America[6]) use publicly available tools. When you hear about "Nessie," pay attention. Nessie stands for the National Survey of Student Engagement (NSSE). In 2017, seventy-two Canadian schools took part in the American-based survey.[7]

C. STUDENTS AND EQUITY, DIVERSITY, AND INCLUSION

Students are diverse and the student population is becoming more diverse. While the percentage of international students is different at each university, and within each province,[8] at Canadian universities collectively, "in 2018–19, international students made up 15.7% of all university enrollments."[9] Immigration patterns in Canada also have an effect on Canadian universities, and children of immigrants are much more likely (2.5 times) to seek post-secondary education than those of Canadian families who have been in Canada for several generations.[10]

A commitment to inclusion must inform university planning and decision-making. It affects everything from communications to academic content. The demographic makeup of your student population and of the community from which your university draws is very important. Understanding that make up, including age; stage of life; socio-economic status; and cultural, ethnic, and religious background should be important to you

---

5 George D Kuh, "Four Ways Boards Can Help Students Succeed," Association of Governing Boards of Universities and Colleges (2011), online: AGB www.agb.org/trusteeship-article/four-ways-boards-can-help-students-succeed.

6 National Survey of Student Engagement, *Engagement Insights: Survey Findings on the Quality of Undergraduate Education — Annual Results 2017* (Bloomington: Indiana University Center for Postsecondary Research, 2017).

7 Mary Dwyer, "National Survey of Student Engagement: Results for Canadian Universities," *Maclean's* (21 December 2018), online: Macleans.ca www.macleans.ca/education/national-survey-of-student-engagement-results-for-canadian-universities.

8 Usher, above note 2 at 20.

9 *Ibid* at 19.

10 Cheryl Foy, "Reflections on the Tragedy of Flight 752," *University Affairs* (17 January 2020), online: University Affairs www.universityaffairs.ca/opinion/in-my-opinion/reflections-on-the-tragedy-of-flight-752.

as a board member as it will help you make informed decisions about the strategic direction for the university, and about the services and supports the university needs to provide to students. The board should understand how student services and supports are prioritized and this priority should be reflected in the university's planning: human resources, strategic, financial, and risk.

D. SOCIAL ISSUES: KEY PRIORITIES

When considering student needs, boards must be aware of the many social issues affecting students. Equity, diversity, and inclusion are mentioned above, and again within this section. Students face mental health challenges and sexual violence. At any given time, there will be aspects of your university's student experience that are more significant than others and the board should pay attention and identify its university's priorities. This chapter does not go into great detail and there are many other books about all of the issues raised below. Other issues will emerge. The intent is to ensure that as a board member you are asking questions about key issues and ensuring that your university is addressing the issues adequately. In 2021 and beyond, I'd suggest that there are several key priorities arising from social issues affecting all university stakeholders and students in particular. (These are not presented in order of importance, and their relative importance should be a decision for the board based on your assessment of the issues most affecting your student.)

1) Student Mental Health

Student mental health is a pressing issue. The statistics show that young people have particular and unique mental health needs.

- Young people aged fifteen to twenty-four are more likely to experience mental illness or substance use disorders or both than any other age group.[11]

---

11 Jennifer Ali, Teresa Janz & Caryn Pearson, "Mental and Substance Use Disorders in Canada," Catalogue no 82-624-X Statistics Canada (September 2013), online: Statistics Canada www150.statcan.gc.ca/n1/en/pub/82-624-x/2013001/article/11855-eng.pdf?st=ckYHAplk.

- In 2016, suicide accounted for 19% of deaths among youth aged ten to fourteen, 29% among youth aged fifteen to nineteen, and 23% among young adults aged twenty to twenty-four.[12]

Student suicide is a tragic and pressing issue, and universities are regularly criticized for failing to provide appropriate mental health support.[13] The board's role is to understand the problem, look at how to address it, and decide how to give priority to this issue. The board should receive regular reports about how plans are being implemented and measured. During budget and financial reviews, particularly during budget cuts, the board should understand the effect of its decisions on student support services.

2) Accommodation of Students with Disabilities

Provincial human rights laws differ across the country. However, all human rights legislation prohibits discrimination on the basis of disability in the provision of services. Higher education is a service and students increasingly need and request accommodations to support them to participate in higher education. These accommodations can range from extended time to write exams or complete assignments to having an assistant present with the student. Universities face resourcing and other challenges in providing the requested accommodations. Again, the board should generally understand the supports and resources for students with disabilities and the challenges faced by the university in meeting these needs.

3) Sexual Violence

Statistics Canada reported in 2020 that one in ten women (11%) experienced sexual violence on campus in the twelve months prior to the survey, as had 4 percent of men.[14] This is troubling for universities. Even more

---

12 "Leading Causes of Death, Total Population, by Age Group," Statistics Canada Table: 13-10-0394-01 (2016), online: Statistics Canada www150.statcan.gc.ca/t1/tbl1/en/tv.action?pid=1310039401.

13 For example, Charlie Fidelman, "Crisis on Campus: Universities Struggle with Students in Distress," *Montreal Gazette* (27 May 2017), online: www.montrealgazette.com/news/local-news/mental-health-on-campus.

14 Marta Burczycka, "Students' Experiences of Unwanted Sexualized Behaviours and Sexual Assault at Postsecondary Schools in the Canadian Provinces, 2019," Statistics Canada (14 September 2020), online: Statistics Canada www150.statcan.gc.ca/n1/pub/85-002-x/2020001/article/00005-eng.htm.

troubling is the fact that students don't report the violence to their institutions. Approximately 75 percent of those experiencing violence didn't report it, and most of those who witness violence don't take action:[15]

> Most students chose not to intervene, seek help or take other action in at least one instance when they witnessed unwanted sexualized behaviours, including 91% of women and 92% of men who witnessed such behaviours. Many women did not act because they felt uncomfortable (48% of those who did not act), because they feared negative consequences (28%), or because they feared for their safety (18%).[16]

As one article notes, "[i]nstitutional responses to sexual violence on Canadian university campuses are now the focus of unprecedented scrutiny by student associations, individual feminists and feminist groups, researchers, the media, and governments."[17] Universities have been accused of having or perpetuating "rape culture."[18] Rape culture can be described "as a culture wherein the dominant attitudes towards rape facilitate, tolerate, and excuse rapists while placing the blame and the onus of rape prevention onto the victims."[19]

The board is responsible for ensuring that your university takes steps to make its campus safe and free from violence. Where or when violence occurs (whether on or off campus and whether it occurred in the past or occurs now), universities are expected to support those affected by sexual violence. Universities must also deal with those accused of perpetrating sexual violence in a procedurally fair way. This involves having policies that deal with all aspects of sexual harassment and violence, ongoing training for staff and students, receiving and processing complaints, procedurally fair investigation, and decision-making processes. The board must take steps to ensure that its university is creating a culture that promotes non-violence and respect, and that discourages and addresses sexual violence, harassment, and discrimination.

---

15 *Ibid*.
16 *Ibid*.
17 Sandrine Ricci & Manon Bergeron, "Tackling Rape Culture in Québec Universities: A Network of Feminist Resistance" (2019) 25 *Violence Against Women* 1290 at 1291.
18 Victoria Wicks, "Does U of T Student Life Condone Rape Culture?" *The Varsity* (31 March 2014), online: www.thevarsity.ca/2014/03/31/does-u-of-t-student-life-condone-rape-culture.
19 Supriya Dwivedi, "Rape Culture Persists in Our Legal System," *Toronto Sun* (4 February 2016), online: www.torontosun.com/2016/02/04/rape-culture-persists-in-our-legal-system/wcm/779c6603-ea1e-46ff-b978-f3e1224b5011.

4) Racism: Anti-Black Racism in 2020

The horrific acts of violence against Black people in 2020 have yet again brought the issue of anti-Black racism to the fore and have resulted in renewed support for the Black Lives Matter movement and demands for real and effective action to combat racism. Canadian universities issued statements denouncing anti-Black and all forms of racism.[20] There appears to be a genuine commitment to action, and it is ultimately the university board's responsibility to ensure action is taken. Stories of marginalization, harassment, violence, and discrimination because of race abound. In her book *They Said This Would Be Fun: Race, Campus Life, and Growing Up*, Eternity Martis details her experiences of racism and sexism, both on campus and in the city of London, Ontario, while a Black student at the University of Western Ontario.[21] A recent article details the racism and sexism experienced by two female graduate students at Queen's University.[22] Universities have faced legal claims and criticism as a result of racial profiling on campus.[23] There is evidence that hate against equity-seeking groups is on the rise.[24]

---

20 "Canadian Institutions Issue Statements Against Racism," Academica Group (3 June 2020), online: Academica Group Inc www.academica.ca/top-ten/canadian-institutions-issue-statements-against-racism.

21 Eternity Martis, *They Said This Would Be Fun: Race, Campus Life, and Growing Up* (Toronto: McClelland & Stewart, 2020).

22 Darryn Davis, "Two Queen's Graduate Students Speak Out About Their Experience with Racism in Kingston," *Global Kingston* (2 October 2020), online: www.msn.com/en-ca/news/world/two-queens-graduate-students-speak-out-about-their-experience-with-racism-in-kingston/ar-BB18DazG?ocid=ientp.

23 For example, "Former Toronto Police Officer Says He Was Racially Profiled by McMaster Security," Academica Group (22 July 2020), online: Academica Group Inc www.academica.ca/top-ten/former-toronto-police-officer-says-he-was-racially-profiled-mcmaster-security; "Student Group Urges UOttawa to end Carding on Campus," Academica Group (27 June 2019), online: Academica Group Inc www.academica.ca/top-ten/student-group-urges-uottawa-end-carding-campus; and "Black UBC Graduate Student Alleges Racial Profiling on Campus," *CBC News* (13 June 2020), online: www.cbc.ca/news/canada/british-columbia/black-ubc-graduate-student-alleges-racial-profiling-on-campus-1.5611316, etc.

24 For example, "Disturbing Data from Statistics Canada Shows Anti-Indigenous Hate Crimes Are on the Rise," *Press Progress* (5 March 2020), online: www.pressprogress.ca/disturbing-data-from-statistics-canada-shows-anti-indigenous-hate-crimes-are-on-the-rise; and Tavia Grant, "Hate Crimes in Canada Rose by 47 Per Cent Last Year: Statscan," *Globe and Mail* (29 November 2018), online: www.theglobeandmail.com/canada/article-hate-crimes-in-canada-rose-by-47-per-cent-last-year-statscan.

5) Racism: Indigenous Students

Included in the students on university campuses is a small and growing number of Indigenous students from diverse backgrounds. Universities Canada reported in 2017 that "an estimated 5% of undergraduate students, 3% of master's and PhD students and 1.4% of full- and part-time faculty on Canadian campuses self-identify as Indigenous."[25] You should understand the needs of, and support services for Indigenous students on your university campuses, as well as the plans to continue to improve those services. Indigenous students also experience hate, racism, and violence in Canadian society; hate crime against Indigenous peoples is on the rise.[26] While 40 percent of students experience food insecurity (financial barriers to securing food), 56.4 percent of Indigenous students and 41.9 percent of racialized students face food insecurity.[27] A number of universities have initiated programs to assist with food insecurity.[28] The calls to action of the Truth and Reconciliation Commission of Canada (TRC) are discussed in more detail below since they include the role of universities in advancing those actions.

E. OTHER THOUGHTS ABOUT STUDENTS

1) Affordability: Tuition and Student Debt

As Alex Usher notes, "[o]ne of the most-watched elements of higher education policy relates to affordability."[29] The affordability picture is a complex one, and boards must avoid being drawn into oversimplifying matters by assuming that tuition is the only measure of affordability. Tuition costs are partially subsidized by student financial aid. Student aid comes in the form of "need-based student aid, tax credits, education savings grants, and institutional scholarships,"[30] and there are other sources. A key measure of

---

25 "Advancing Reconciliation through Higher Education: 2017 Survey Findings," Universities Canada (April 2018), online: www.univcan.ca/wp-content/uploads/2018/10/Indigenous_survey_findings_2017_factsheet_25Apr_.pdf.
26 *Ibid* at 25.
27 Drew Silverthorn, *Hungry for Knowledge: Assessing the Prevalence of Student Food Insecurity on Five Canadian Campuses* (Toronto: Meal Exchange, 2016) at 16.
28 Anqi Shen, "Universities Take Steps to Tackle Food Insecurity on Campus," *University Affairs* (7 March 2019), online: University Affairs www.universityaffairs.ca/news/news-article/universities-take-steps-to-tackle-food-insecurity-on-campus.
29 Usher, above note 2 at 49.
30 *Ibid* at 57.

affordability is the amount of student debt students carry at graduation. According to Usher's analysis student debt has been flat since 2010. He notes that "the majority of Canadian college and undergraduate students do not incur any debt at all."[31] He further writes, "despite all the frequent platitudes about 'ever-increasing student debt,' the massive increase in student aid ... has in fact brought the student debt problem relatively under control," noting that surveys from 2006 forward peg student debt between $25,000 and $30,000.[32] Noting that all of this information interprets the national picture, it is valuable for board members to understand the financial situation of its own students: in addition to tuition information, they should seek to understand financial supports available to students, as well as how many students are using them.

2) Competition for Students

While universities cooperate extensively in research and academic programs and in many other ways, universities also compete for students; this competition changes the dynamic between the student and the university. Universities must "sell" themselves and their academic programs to the students, and then they have to deliver on all aspects of the sales assurances. Students (along with their parents) evaluate their education in terms of employability and earnings potential. For the board, this dynamic creates both strategic opportunity and risk. From the strategic opportunity perspective, it is important to understand how your president and leadership team are creating and implementing a strategy to allow the university to "sell" and differentiate itself. What is the university's value proposition to the students and how does it deliver against that value proposition? How are academic programs innovative and attractive? How do students feel about tuition levels and how does your university's tuition compare to that charged by others for the same programs?

3) Educational Malpractice Claims by Students

From the risk perspective, your board should understand that "educational malpractice" claims are on the rise. When student expectations are disappointed because of misrepresentations or overselling and under

---

31   *Ibid* at 60.
32   *Ibid*.

delivery, students sue their universities. The Canadian Universities Reciprocal Insurance Exchange (CURIE) (a key source of insurance coverage for about two-thirds of Canadian universities) notes that these claims, also known as "failure to educate" claims, represent approximately 84 percent of all errors and omissions liability claims.[33] According to CURIE, failure to educate claims include:

- Breach of contract;
- Negligent misrepresentation (including misrepresentations in student calendars or student literature);
- Sufficiency of academic accommodation;
- Negligent supervision and training;
- Bias/bad faith, racism, or personal conflicts in clinical rotations;
- Breach of fiduciary duty;
- Failure to grant degree/degree requirements;
- Decisions regarding student status;
- Improper advice;
- Conspiracy to injure;
- Defamation (both online and traditional modes);
- Alleged racism or discrimination based on country of origin or other protected grounds;
- Breach of duty of care;
- Harassment;
- Alleged bias/discrimination in evaluation and/or appeals procedures;
- Conflict between student and faculty/supervisor;
- Delayed graduation/delayed entry into workforce due to wrongdoing of university;
- Administrative errors;
- Failing to provide the necessary tools, feedback, and/or professional services for a successful educational experience.[34]

While these claims are often not successful, they are costly to litigate and they potentially have reputational consequences for the university. University boards should understand the nature and extent of student disputes with the university. To the extent that there are patterns, these disputes will

---

33 "Failure to Educate ... Who is Failing Whom?" CURIE (2015), online: CURIE www.curie.org/sites/default/files/2015%20Educational%20Malpractice%20Bulletin%20-%20April%2015%202015.pdf at 2.
34 *Ibid* at 1.

point to a gap between what is promised and delivered by the university to its students. These gaps should interest the board from both the strategic and risk perspectives.

4) Alumni

When students graduate and become alumni, they remain an important university stakeholder group. Many alumni retain an interest in the activities of their former university. They may remain involved with the school in various capacities — serving as board members, or on advisory committees at the university, faculty or department level. They may serve as mentors and advisors; they may come back to the university to teach or facilitate educational experiences in their own businesses and workplaces. Many become donors to the university and, recognizing the importance of alumni to university fundraising, most universities spend significant time and resources to retain a relationship with alumni.

Boards should understand that decisions taken by the university, particularly those that affect the university's brand and reputation, affect alumni. It is for this reason that universities include alumni when they consult on key decisions anticipated to affect them. For example, the Faculty of Law at Queen's University included alumni among those it consulted before changing the name of the Law School.[35] Alumni may also react to decisions made by the university — alumni of St. Francis Xavier University recently participated with students in expressing their concerns about a COVID waiver the university asked its returning students to sign.[36] Queen's University alumni reacted negatively when the university fired a long-time track coach.[37] Board decisions may also attract alumni attention — when McGill University's Board of Governors decided not to divest

---

35 See Queen's University, "Building Name Consultation Process," online: https://law.queensu.ca/about/consultation.

36 Canadian Press, "Students at St. Francis Xavier University Protest Wording of COVID-19 Waiver" *Lethbridge News* (13 July 2020), online: https://lethbridgenewsnow.com/2020/07/13/students-at-st-francis-xavier-university-protest-wording-of-covid-19-waiver.

37 Michael Doyle, "Queen's University Sees Fallout from Track Coach's Firing" *Globe and Mail* (20 February 2020), online: www.theglobeandmail.com/canada/article-queens-university-sees-fallout-from-track-coachs-firing/.

from fossil fuel companies, some alumni decided to return their diplomas.[38] Some alumni at Nova Scotia College of Art and Design protested when the board terminated the president's employment.[39] It is important to consider the effects of board decisions on alumni, to consult alumni when appropriate, and to have a communication plan for alumni where alumni support of board decisions is required.

F. CONCLUSION

Students are the primary stakeholders for universities, and your university board must work to understand the interests, needs, and expectations of the students on your campus. Keeping in mind that the board's role is not an operational role, the board needs an understanding of student demographics, profiles, issues, and interests in order to fulfil its role in ensuring that the university's strategic and academic direction is appropriate and that a culture and environment that supports student learning exists. There is much to know in order to fulfil this aspect of the mandate and the board must remain focused on all aspects of university culture and student life.

Boards should keep in mind that if the university is successful at maintaining a relationship with its graduating students, those students become alumni who remain involved with the university. As such, alumni are another important university stakeholder. Boards should understand the university's approach to alumni relations, should understand when board and university decisions may affect alumni, and should take alumni interests into account.

---

38 "McGill Board Stands Firm on Fossil Fuel Investments" *CBC News* (11 April 2016), online: www.cbc.ca/news/canada/montreal/mcgill-board-stands-firm-on-fossil-fuel-investments-1.3529994.

39 See, as an example of the nature of the protest, Mark Denil, "An Open Letter about the State of NSCAD from a Concerned Alumnus" *The Nova Scotia Advocate* (14 October 2020), online: https://nsadvocate.org/2020/10/14/an-open-letter-about-the-state-of-nscad-from-a-concerned-alumnus.

CHAPTER 6

Key Internal Stakeholders: Faculty

A. BACKGROUND INFORMATION

There are approximately 47,000 faculty at Canada's universities.[1] Faculty are essential to universities because they engage in the primary work of the universities—research and teaching. Matters of concern for the board relating to faculty include quality and productivity and the measurement of the same, the implications of the university's faculty demographics, faculty morale, alignment between faculty profile, faculty research, and faculty expertise with university strategic direction and student demand, and labour relations issues.

Statistics Canada breaks down full-time faculty into four basic categories. This is the breakdown as of 2018–2019:

---

1 "Number of Full-time Teaching Staff at Canadian Universities, by Rank, Sex" Table: 37-10-0076-01 Statistics Canada (2019), online: Statistics Canada www150.statcan.gc.ca/t1/tbl1/en/tv.action?pid=3710007601.

Table 6.1 Full-Time Faculty Categories[2]

Rank	2018–2019
Total rank	46,443
Full professor	16,743
Associate professor	15,981
Assistant professor	8,661
Rank or level below assistant professor, including lecturers, instructors, and other faculty	3,963
Other (not elsewhere classified)	1,095

As indicated in the table above, faculty have different ranks. The meaning of these ranks, and indeed, the number of ranks, may differ a little from university to university. There are also differences in ranking systems between North America and Europe. In some cases, the ranking and categories are established by practice, in others by policy,[3] and in others it is set out in the collective agreement.[4] There are both full-time and part-time faculty.

In addition to the groups above, there is a group of faculty members that exists in some institutions, known as "clinical faculty." Clinical faculty are instructors who also hold appointments in clinical settings (such as hospitals) and also within a university affiliated with the clinical settings. These types of faculty members are most prominent in universities with medical schools, but may also exist in schools with nursing or other health science programs.[5] Unique issues arise with these faculty members because, although they work within the university, their primary affiliation is elsewhere. They often do not receive compensation from the university.

---

2 *Ibid.*
3 For example, Terry Lavender, "U of T Introduces New Teaching Stream Professorial Ranks" *U of T News* (10 July 2015), online: www.utoronto.ca/news/u-t-introduces-new-teaching-stream-professorial-ranks.
4 For example, The University of Ontario Institute of Technology and The University of Ontario Institute of Technology Faculty Association, "Collective Agreement Between The University of Ontario Institute of Technology and The University of Ontario Institute of Technology Faculty Association" (4 March 2019), online: https://shared.ontariotechu.ca/shared/department/hr/Working-at-UOIT/faculty-association---collective-agreement,-effective-march-4,-2019-to-june-30,-2021.pdf at 16–21.
5 For example, University of Toronto, "Policy for Clinical Faculty" (16 December 2004), online: https://governingcouncil.utoronto.ca/secretariat/policies/clinical-faculty-policy-december-16-2004.

B. THE WORK OF FACULTY

Faculty work is divided into three main areas: (1) teaching, (2) scholarship (also described as "research" or "scholarly activity"), and (3) service (both within and external to the university). The time spent on each of these areas by an individual faculty member may be established within a collective agreement or may be allocated annually by a dean. In 2014, the Higher Education Quality Council of Ontario (HEQCO) noted that for tenured or tenure-track faculty, Ontario "universities generally adhere to a faculty workload distribution of 40% teaching, 40% research and 20% service."[6]

Issues of interest to university boards include quality of faculty work and the assessment of that quality. Universities need high-quality teaching, but how is that assessed?[7] How is productivity measured? Note that in the HEQCO article cited above, the authors concluded that improvements in productivity are possible with increased attention to faculty productivity:

> From our data, we estimate that about 27% of faculty members in economics and 7% of faculty members in chemistry have neither published in peer-reviewed journals nor received a Tri-Council grant in a three-year period. These research non-active faculty members teach, on average, 0.9 courses more in economics and 0.5 courses more in chemistry than their research-active colleagues.
>
> Extrapolating from our sample, we suggest that if research non-active faculty members were to teach twice the teaching load of their research-active colleagues (as might be suggested by the typical 40%-40%-20% expectation of effort across teaching, research and service), the overall teaching capacity of the full-time professoriate in Ontario would be increased by about 10%, a teaching impact equivalent to adding about 1,500 additional faculty members across the province.[8]

As universities face issues of financial sustainability, evaluating faculty productivity will be of significant interest to university boards. It is important that board members understand the critical role that faculty play within a

---

6   Martin Hicks & Linda Jonker, *Teaching Loads and Research Outputs of Ontario University Faculty Members: Implications for Productivity and Differentiation* (Toronto: Higher Education Quality Council of Ontario, 2014) at 7.

7   For example, Sarah Forgie, Janice Miller-Young & Melina Sinclair, "Teaching Excellence and How It Is Awarded: A Canadian Case Study" (2020) 50 *Canadian Journal of Higher Education* 40.

8   *Ibid.*

university. It is important for planning and oversight that board members understand the constraints within the university's relationship to faculty. The rest of this chapter focuses on some of the key faculty-related issues with which universities grapple and about which boards should be aware.

C. SYSTEMIC BARRIERS FOR WOMEN AND RACIALIZED FACULTY

When considering faculty demographics, among the key issues are underrepresentation of women and equity-seeking groups, particularly racialized candidates. This is an issue for faculty, but also an issue for students seeking role models within the university as, for example, the estimated percentage of visible minority students in first year is about 40 percent.[9] Visible minority faculty are much fewer in number, as White male faculty "outnumber visible minorities and women at Canadian universities from coast to coast."[10] As Statistics Canada notes:

> Women represent a growing share of university faculty, accounting for nearly 40% of all full-time teaching employees at universities, up markedly from 12.8% in 1970/1971.
>
> The university workforce is getting older. While 60% of university staff were aged under 40 in 1970/1971, that share had fallen to 15% by 2016/2017. At the other end of the age spectrum, the opposite occurred. While less than 1% of staff were aged 65 and older in 1970/1971, this share had risen to more than 10% in 2016/2017.[11]

While women represent nearly 40 percent of faculty, they represent a much smaller percentage (28.8%) of full professors.[12] Universities are expected to have gender balance and diversity within their workforces. As will be discussed in more detail later, the Canadian federal government plays a

---

9 Anya Zoledziowski, "Lack of Faculty Diversity Can Affect Studies and Career Aspirations," *Globe and Mail* (18 October 2017), online: www.theglobeandmail.com/news/national/education/canadian-university-report/lack-of-faculty-diversity-can-affect-studies-and-career-aspirations/article36637410.
10 *Ibid.*
11 "UCASS Revisited," Statistics Canada (18 January 2018), online: Statistics Canada www.statcan.gc.ca/eng/blog/cs/ucass-revisited.
12 "How Far Have We Come: Representation of Women Among Full-Time University Faculty," Statistics Canada (5 March 2020), online: www150.statcan.gc.ca/n1/pub/11-627-m/11-627-m2020021-eng.htm.

significant role in funding university research. One of the mechanisms by which research is funded is through the Canada Research Chairs Program (CRCP). Through this program, the federal government hands out about $300 million annually to approximately 2,300 researchers at universities across Canada.[13] Through the implementation of its Equity, Diversity and Inclusion Plan, the CRCP is requiring institutions to adopt a variety of employment equity best practices and to report on the results of these practices.[14]

There isn't an abundance of information on the racial composition of faculty. Information from one Canadian study published in *The Equity Myth* confirms that "racialized and Indigenous faculty members are under-represented and they experience racism."[15] A survey was undertaken in 2019 by Statistics Canada to fill data gaps with respect to equity, diversity, and inclusion among university and college faculty and post-doctoral student concludes the following:

- Of those surveyed, about one-third identify with at least two of the following diversity groups: visible minority, Indigenous identity, self-reported disability, sexual orientation, and use of official languages. Those studying for their PhDs and post-doctoral fellows are more likely to identify with more diversity groups.
- The representation of male and female respondents is roughly equal at universities (51% male and 48% female). Women account for slightly more of those studying for their PhDs (52%) and a significantly lower number of those who are post-doctoral fellows (41%).
- Gender-diverse respondents were represented as follows:
  » Faculty — 0.2%
  » Post-doctoral fellows — 1.2%
  » PhD students — 0.7%
- Gender-diverse individuals (41%) and women (20%) are much more likely than men (11%) to have experienced unfair treatment or discrimination due to at least one diversity characteristic.

---

13 Government of Canada, Canada Research Chairs, online: www.chairs-chaires.gc.ca/home-accueil-eng.aspx.
14 "Equity, Diversity and Inclusion Action Plan," Canada Research Chairs Program (May 2017), online: Government of Canada www.chairs-chaires.gc.ca/program-programme/equity-equite/action_plan-plan_action-eng.aspx.
15 Frances Henry et al, *The Equity Myth: Racialization and Indigeneity at Canadian Universities* (Vancouver: UBC Press, 2017) at 301.

- Tenured faculty are less diverse and more likely to be male:
  » Males—43% are tenured
  » Females—32% are tenured
  » Indigenous—21% are tenured (compared with 37% of non-Indigenous faculty)
- Percentages of groups receiving funding:
  » Male faculty—44%
  » Visible minority faculty—44%
  » Women faculty —40%
  » Indigenous faculty—37%
  » Non-Indigenous faculty—42%
  » Faculty self-reporting disability—38%
- Faculty not reporting disability—42%[16]

In order to understand how diverse the faculty is, reliable data must be secured, not just about the university workforce, but also about the communities from which that workforce is drawn. More attention should be paid to this work. In the interim, there is sufficient evidence of systemic barriers that the board should ensure that there is an equity, diversity, and inclusion plan in place to support inclusion across faculty ranks.

D. FACULTY AGE DEMOGRAPHICS

The age demographic of faculty has broad implications for universities, and for boards from a salary expense perspective and from faculty composition and renewal perspectives. As noted by H Weingarten et al, "full-time faculty are the single largest employee group at universities and represent 34% of total operating expenditures for Ontario institutions."[17] Weingarten et al address the implications of the abolition of mandatory retirement:

> But assuming, for illustration purposes, that mandatory retirement had not been eliminated, that faculty had continued to retire at age 65, and

---

16 "Survey of Postsecondary Faculty and Researchers, 2019," Statistics Canada (22 October 2020), online: Statistics Canada www150.statcan.gc.ca/n1/daily-quotidien/200922/dq200922a-eng.htm.

17 Harvey P Weingarten, Linda Jonker, Amy Kaufman & Martin Hicks, "University Sustainability: Expenditures" (Toronto: Higher Education Quality Council of Ontario, 2018), online: https://heqco.ca/pub/university-sustainability-expenditures at 14.

that they had been replaced by faculty in the 35 and younger age bracket, we calculate that:

- Universities could have maintained the same overall full-time faculty complement as today, but at a salary savings of $89 million in 2016
- The overall age composition of Ontario faculty ... would have remained much more stable over the period 2005 to 2016, with more newly minted PhDs (up to 1,239) hired into faculty positions.
- Alternatively, for the same annual salary expenditure as today, universities could have increased their total faculty complement by 781, or 6% in 2016.[18]

Understanding the demographic makeup at your university will give you insight into key strategic issues affecting the university, as well as into the parameters within which the senior leadership team of your university must make decisions.

E. UNIONIZATION

Board members should understand the unionization profile of university employees and should understand the labour relations environment, as well as the key issues for the bargaining units. The approval of bargaining mandates and ratification of collective agreements falls to the board or to one of its committees or to both. As Ian Austin and Glen Jones note:

> In Canada, higher education is one of the most heavily unionized of all sectors, and the vast majority of faculty are members of recognized institution-based trade unions. In addition, sessional/adjunct faculty, teaching assistants, research assistants, support staff and many other categories of workers may be members of separate labour unions at the same university.[19]

Statistics Canada includes universities in the public sector and reports unionization rates for the sector of 75 percent.[20] This rate is in stark contrast to that in the United States, which reports faculty unionization at approximately 27 percent.[21] There is more on the role of faculty associations in the governance of the university in Chapter 14.

---

18   *Ibid* at 21–22.
19   Ian Austin & Glen A Jones, *Governance of Higher Education: Global Perspectives, Theories, and Practices* (New York: Routledge, 2016) at 140.
20   "Union Status by Industry," Statistics Canada Table: 14-10-0132-01 (2019), online: Statistics Canada www150.statcan.gc.ca/t1/tbl1/en/tv.action?pid=1410013201.
21   Austin & Jones, above note 19 at 140.

F. TENURE AND PROMOTION

This section of the chapter covers the concept of tenure, how is it obtained, and the board's role in tenure. As the board of governors typically plays a role in tenure or promotion, it is important for board members to understand it. Very simply put, tenure is a form of "job security [for] academic peers."[22] Effectively, a tenured appointment can only be terminated in the very limited circumstance of just cause. While there may have been negotiated terminations in the past in Canada, I believe there has been only one arbitration case in Canada upholding the decision to terminate a tenured professor for cause.[23] Gerald Walton notes that tenure is "widely misunderstood as job protection even by [tenured faculty]" and thus offers a more nuanced definition: "Contrary to the job-protection assumption . . . tenure is the scholarly triptych of 'intellectual independence, collective autonomy, and the time and financial security needed to carry on scholarly and scientific work.'"[24] It is important that board members don't oversimplify or misunderstand tenure. While tenure represents a constraint to universities looking to reduce or reallocate faculty resources, it also underpins academic activities central to the contributions make to our society. In Chapter 11, we'll be looking at the concept of academic freedom and will revisit the role of tenure in protecting academic freedom.

Teaching staff can be promoted through ranks. Academic ranks can be tenured, working toward tenure ("tenure track"), or outside of the tenure process completely. Looking at the four categories identified by Statistics Canada in Table 6.1, both full professor and associate professor are likely to have tenure. An assistant professor is likely to be working toward tenure. Those below the rank of assistant professor are likely to be outside of the tenure process.

It takes an academic three to seven years after receiving a doctorate (PhD), to earn tenure;[25] the average is 6.2 years.[26] Not all academics are successful at achieving tenure. As one article notes:

---

22 *Ibid* at 130.
23 *University of Ottawa v Association of Professors of the University of Ottawa*, 2014 CanLII 100735 (Ont Lab Arb Bd).
24 Gerald Walton, "Academic Underperformers Must Be Called Out," *University Affairs* (9 January 2017), online: University Affairs www.universityaffairs.ca/opinion/in-my-opinion/academic-underperformers-must-called.
25 Pamela Gravestock & Emily Gregor Greenleaf, "Overview of Tenure and Promotion Policies Across Canada," University of Toronto (2008), online: University of Toronto https://gov.viu.ca/sites/default/files/overviewoftppoliciesincanada.pdf.
26 "Survey of Postsecondary Faculty and Researchers, 2019," above note 16.

In Canada, the performance of new tenure-track academics is evaluated at least once (and sometimes annually) in the early years of their appointments, culminating in a more extensive appraisal (the "tenure review") after about five or six years that will determine whether the individual is given a permanent appointment or a one-year terminal contract. The review process extends over an academic year or longer, requires considerable documentation and the labour of many people, and often involves external as well as internal assessors. "Going up for tenure" is not optional and lack of success, appeals aside, means losing one's job. Because the stakes are so high, the prospect of being reviewed for tenure comes to dominate the lives of early-career tenure-track faculty.[27]

The tenure process differs by institution, and in many institutions, the board of governors plays a role in approving tenure appointments:

> Tenure and promotion policies and processes are normally articulated in collective agreements between faculty associations/unions and the institution or its board of governors. These procedures normally begin with a review at the departmental level and subsequently reviewed at the divisional/decanal level and finally by either the board and/or the president/rector/chancellor. At every stage of the process, the policy will normally include opportunities for appeal or grievance which is usually facilitated by the faculty association or union. The tenure process typically also includes a pre-tenure review (normally in the 3rd year of appointment) that measures the candidate's progress and promise in relation to institutional expectations for tenure. With the granting of tenure, Assistant Professors are normally promoted to the rank of Associate Professor.[28]

1) Tenure and the Board

The two key considerations for the board with regard to tenure are understanding the tenure process and the board's role, and understanding the implications of tenure as a part of university structure. For the purposes of the tenure discussion, boards should understand that their role in tenure is generally delegated to them under the university's applicable legislation. Therefore, boards should be familiar with the legal documents under which

---

27 Sandra Acker & Michelle Webber, "Discipline and Publish: The Tenure Review Process in Ontario Universities" in Lynette Shultz & Melody Viczko, *Assembling and Governing the Higher Education Institution* (London: Palgrave Macmillan, 2016) at 235.
28 Gravestock & Gregor Greenleaf above note 25 at 4.

the board is delegated its powers. For older universities like Queen's University at Kingston, the originating document is the university's charter. For most universities in Canada, the power is derived from legislation. In some provinces (such as Alberta—see the *Post-Secondary Learning Act*,[29] and British Columbia—see the *University Act*[30]) the legislation may be general, and applicable to all post-secondary institutions in the province. For most universities, however, the university is created by way of its own legislation. See the following examples in Table 6.2.

Table 6.2 Board Delegated Authority over Tenure — Examples

University	Applicable Legislation	Relevant Excerpt
Ontario Tech University	*University of Ontario Institute of Technology Act, 2002*, SO 2002, c 8, Sched O	Under section 9 "Powers and Duties of the Board": "(e) to appoint, promote, suspend and remove members of the teaching staff and of the administrative staff of the university."
University of Saskatchewan	*University of Saskatchewan Act, 1995*, SS 1995, c U-6.1	Under section 49 "Responsibilities and Powers of the Board": "(j) subject to sections 50 and 51, appoint the president, the vice-president or vice-presidents, the secretary, the faculty members and any other officers and employees that are required to be appointed by this Act or that it considers necessary for the purposes of the university, fix their salaries or remuneration and define their duties and terms of office or employment."
British Columbia's universities	*University Act*, RSBC 1996, c 468 (general legislation applicable to British Columbia's universities)	Under section 27 "Powers of Board" see subsection (g) "subject to section 28, to appoint the president of the university, deans of all faculties, the librarian, the registrar, the bursar, the professors, associate professors, assistant professors, lecturers, instructors and other members of the teaching staff of the university, and the officers and employees the board considers necessary for the purpose of the university, and to set their salaries or remuneration, and to define their duties and their tenure of office or employment."

29   SA 2003, c P-19.5.
30   RSBC 1996, c 468.

The tenure process is a process of evaluation of the work of a faculty member by a committee of colleagues. As noted above, all or part of the process may be enshrined in a collective agreement. The recommendation of the collegial committee typically proceeds to review by provost or president or both. After completion of an extensive internal process, and under the university's legislation, the president is often charged with recommending appointments, promotions, or tenure to the board. Given the collegial nature of the internal process, if the board has a role in approving tenure appointments, it should rarely, if ever, exercise its discretion to reject a tenure recommendation, and then only if it becomes aware that the tenure-selection process has deviated from accepted university practice.[31] Decisions to recommend a denial of tenure have been considered by Canadian courts.[32]

2) University Structure and Tenure

Tenured faculty have job security. This security may be enhanced by provisions of the collective agreement. There are good reasons for the protected status of tenured faculty (see Chapter 11, Section G). The drawback, from an organizational perspective, of this protected status is that there is a rigidity to the organizational structure of universities. For example, let's take fictional university YourU. YourU has twenty-five tenured faculty teaching journalism. Many of the faculty are experts in traditional forms of print, radio, and television journalism but none study or work in new forms of digital journalism or social media. The university would like to create a digital journalism program. The university's budget is very limited. The faculty association collective agreement has a no lay-off clause in it and a process related to the closure of programs that is protracted and contains various protective provisions for affected faculty. In this scenario, elements of which can be seen in universities across the country, YourU has limited ability to build a digital journalism program quickly, and very little ability to discontinue the traditional journalism program. It must rely on faculty cooperation and support to modify its existing program, which may or may not be easy to secure.

---

31 Peter MacKinnon, *University Leadership and Public Policy in the Twenty-First Century: A President's Perspective* (Toronto: University of Toronto Press, 2014) at 101–7.

32 For those interested in reading more about the tensions and interests underlying these disputes, see Peter MacKinnon, "Let's Make a Deal: On Governance, Collegial Management, and Collective Bargaining" in MacKinnon, *ibid* at ch 6.

Board members from the private sector often do not understand the extent to which change within universities depends upon the goodwill and support of faculty. Similarly, a university board facing the need for significant budget cuts should understand that tenure and unionization mean that faculty cuts will be virtually impossible without the cooperation of the faculty bargaining unit.

3) Part-Time Faculty

Universities also rely on part-time faculty who may be described in a number of ways, including as lecturers, instructors, sessionals, limited-term appointees, or adjuncts. The proportion of part-time faculty to full-time faculty in the ranks described above has been increasing. As one article notes:

> In 2016–17, 38,681 faculty appointments, or 53.60 per cent, were contract positions compared to 33,490 tenured and tenure-track appointments.
>
> Among contract faculty, part-time appointments predominate, accounting for nearly 80 per cent of all contract appointments in 2016–17.[33]

The board should understand the reasons for increasing reliance on contract faculty at your university. Further, the board should understand that this increased reliance gives rise to matters of concern to the board.

There are two key issues that arise from increasing reliance on contract faculty. The first issue is a labour relations issue that has been taken up by faculty bargaining units and the Canadian Association of University Teachers (CAUT).[34] While contract faculty permit the university flexibility, some are concerned about the working conditions for those in what has been called the "precariat."[35] The work of these people is precarious — meaning occasional, temporary, and unpredictable — and often less well paid than that of their full-time counterparts. The board has an interest in workplace culture and faculty labour relations.

---

33 Chandra Pasma & Erika Shaker, "Contract U: Contract Faculty Appointments at Canadian Universities" (Ottawa: Canadian Centre for Policy Alternatives, 2018) at 5.

34 Louise Birdsell Bauer & Karen Foster, "Out of the Shadows: Experiences of Contract Academic Staff," Canadian Association of University Teachers (September 2018), online: CAUT www.caut.ca/sites/default/files/cas_report.pdf.

35 Kane X Faucher, "Welcome to a New Space for Adjunct Faculty," *University Affairs* (5 February 2014), online: University Affairs www.universityaffairs.ca/career-advice/contractually-bound/contractually-bound-welcome-to-a-new-space-for-adjunct-faculty.

A second key area of concern for the board is the effect on academic quality and understanding the effect of the use of contract faculty on the quality and continuity of the student academic experience. Boards should also be concerned about the reputational issues arising from reliance on contract faculty.

G. CONCLUSION

Faculty are key stakeholders crucial to the central mission of universities. Their teaching and research work is the lifeblood of the university and they expect their importance to be recognized and reflected through inclusion in governance and consultation on key decisions. It is important for boards to have a sense of faculty demographics, the issues about which your faculty are concerned, areas of tension and conflict, as well as the achievements of your faculty.

CHAPTER 7

Key Internal Stakeholders: Administration

University administrators are all those employees whose functions support directly or indirectly the teaching and scholarship activities of the university. Those functions include human resources, student support and services, finance, legal, facilities management, research support, campus security, campus health, advancement (fundraising), communications, government relations, and many more. Administration is divided into two classes: academic administrators and administrators. Academic administrators typically are faculty members who have risen through the ranks to take on the leadership role of an academic function within the university. The president is the most senior administrator presiding over both academic and administrative activities of the university. The leadership team is that group of employees comprising both academic and administrative leaders reporting to the president, and reporting to those who report to the president. Administrative employees employed in university support functions — such as human resources, student support and services, finance, legal, and so on — are similar to employees working in those roles across other sectors. The president and the leadership team have an important role to play in the governance of the university.

A. ORGANIZATIONAL STRUCTURE AND ITS IMPORTANCE TO THE BOARD

The organizational structure of universities differs from school to school. It is generally important for boards to understand organizational structure. Additionally, from a board perspective, looking at which functions have been chosen for representation on the senior leadership team can tell you about the administration's priorities. An examination of the senior administrative positions can be extremely valuable to the work you do as a board member. For example, one question I often ask is why we don't see the human resources function represented more often at the leadership table, given that universities are essentially a people "business." Instead, human resources often reports through a vice-president of finance and administration or, if the department is bifurcated, academic human resources (called academic affairs or academic labour relations) may report through the provost.[1] Additionally, if equity, diversity, and inclusion are important, where are they represented within the organizational structure? Assessing the organizational structure—determining who has a leadership role and who doesn't—will help the board gauge which functions are prioritized, and where there are potential gaps in stakeholder perspectives or a lack of focus in a strategic area.

B. KEY ROLES

The positions outlined below are commonly seen at Canadian universities.

1) Chancellor

The chancellor of most universities is described as the head of the school in title only. The chancellor is a volunteer, typically a board member (who may or may not participate in board work), and has a key role to play in ceremonial matters at universities. The following description of the role found on Queen's University's website is illustrative:

> The Chancellor is the highest officer and the ceremonial head of the University. Modelled after similar positions at Scottish universities, the office was created in 1874 and first filled in 1877, although it was only enshrined in law in 1882 after a convoluted process (see Royal Charter).

---

1   Note that the University of Toronto has a vice-president human resources and equity, and the University of British Columbia has a vice-president human resources.

The Chancellor presides over convocations, confers degrees, and chairs the annual meetings of the University Council. He or she is an ex-officio voting member of the Board of Trustees and many of its committees.[2]

2) President and Vice-Chancellor

There is a debate over calling the senior executive role within a university the chief executive officer, which implies that the person in this role runs the business side of things, rather than the academic. Many argue that the president is not the chief executive officer but is, rather, the chief academic officer. This role is occasionally also called "principal."[3] The president is the executive leader of the university and all employees at the university report to this person. The president sits below the chancellor and so typically also has the title "vice-chancellor." The president is usually a member of the board and of the academic governing body, and is often the chair of the latter. It is the role of the board to hire, manage, and terminate the employment of the president. For this reason, there's more context on the role and the challenges associated with the role in Chapter 15.

3) Chief Academic Officer

The chief academic officer reports to the president and bears various titles that usually include "vice-president academic" often before or after "provost." Where the chief executive officer is called the "principal," the chief academic officer will be the "vice-principal academic." As this role is responsible for the entire academic function, it has been described as the vice-president who is "first among equals."[4] Although faculty operate very independently, from an organizational perspective they report through their respective department chairs and deans, and ultimately to the chief academic officer (who, in turn, and as noted above, reports to the president).

The portfolio of the chief academic officer is broad and varied and includes academic strategic direction, hiring, performance management and termination of the faculty deans, faculty relations, faculty professional

---

2 "Chancellors," Queen's Encyclopedia (n.d.), online: Queen's University www.queensu.ca/encyclopedia/c/chancellors. Chancellors, Queen's Encyclopedia.
3 See, for example: Queen's University at Kingston, and McGill University.
4 James Martin & James E Samels, *First Among Equals: The Role of the Chief Academic Officer* (Baltimore: Johns Hopkins University Press, 1997).

development, academic quality, oversight of accreditation of professional programs, education and technology, student life issues, diversity and inclusion, enrolment management, financial management and budgeting, and more.

4) Chief Research Officer

Most universities have a separate executive responsible for overseeing the research activity of the university.[5] The titles that this person has will include "vice-president research." The chief research officer may also have responsibility for university innovation and thus "and innovation" added to the title. The responsibility for innovation is a responsibility to promote innovation in research and to ensure that innovation occurring at the university is appropriately communicated to the external world. As noted above, the faculty who perform the research (with the assistance of research assistants, graduate and undergraduate students, and others) are the organizational responsibility of the chief academic officer, and so do not report to the chief research officer.

The chief research officer is responsible for the strategic direction of research at the university, for overseeing research activity, and for providing support to researchers. The role also involves responsibility for research ethics compliance. Any research projects that involve animal or human research must undergo an ethics review to ensure compliance with accepted standards. There are a wide variety of activities required to support the work of researchers. Assisting and supporting faculty to secure research funding is a key part of the chief research officer's role. Funding is secured through contracts with government and third parties, and ensuring effective contract management and contractual compliance is another key role for the chief research officer.

It is important that board members understand that while universities pay faculty salaries and provide the faculty with research facilities (offices, laboratories, and equipment), most research is only possible through external funding. The federal government is a significant source of research funding, and partnerships with all levels of government, and other public- and private-sector organizations are also very important to research. A primary focus of the chief research officer is, therefore, enhancing the university's reputation and ranking in research. A university's research contribution is a

---

5   Note that the University of Prince Edward Island has a vice-president academic and research, and that other universities may have the same position.

key aspect of its reputation. There is more about university ranking in Chapter 10, but suffice it to say here that there are a number of global university-ranking initiatives and that their primary focus is on "research productivity, impact, and excellence as lead comparisons of [university] quality."[6]

5) Chief Financial Officer

Every institution will have a vice-president in charge of finances. In a few universities, this is a standalone role bearing the title "chief financial officer."[7] However, in many universities, this role will also include responsibility for some aspect of operations as well. Titles vary from "vice-president finance and administration,"[8] "vice-president administration and operations,"[9] "vice-president finance and operations,"[10] and "vice-president finance and service"[11] to other titles. As you consider the scope of operations at universities, you will begin to appreciate that universities are financially complex. The responsibilities include payroll, expenses, procurement, accounts payable, and accounts receivable (all students have accounts). From a real property perspective, universities are owners, landlords, and tenants. From a research perspective, universities typically provide financial supports (research accounting, procurement, accounts payable, etc.) to faculty in order to ensure compliance with the terms of research grants. There are investments, pension funds, and endowment funds. For more on university finances, see Chapter 16.

6) Advancement Executive

If you are coming from the private sector, the title of this executive (most often "vice-president advancement" or "vice-president external relations") may be an unfamiliar one. Within universities, the advancement function incorporates a number of activities significant to the university and highly relevant to the board's mandate. These activities typically include public relations, media relations, government relations, alumni relations, publications, marketing (brand and website), and fundraising (also called development).

---

6 Peter MacKinnon, *University Leadership and Public Policy in the Twenty-First Century: A President's Perspective* (Toronto: University of Toronto Press, 2014).
7 See University of Toronto and Ontario Tech University.
8 See University of Prince Edward Island, University of New Brunswick, and Queen's University at Kingston.
9 See Ryerson University.
10 See University of Victoria.
11 See University of Calgary.

Although universities get a significant proportion of their operating expenses from the provincial government and from tuition, fundraising plays a key part in enabling universities to offer student financial assistance in its various forms. This fundraising is also critical to support research and the university's ability to develop and refurbish its capital assets.[12]

7) Governance Professional

The job of managing university governance falls within the responsibility of the university secretariat, which is overseen by the university secretary (who also may be called the "secretary general"). This role is comparable to, although generally much more demanding and complex than, a corporate secretarial role. This is a key function within a university, and the university secretary typically reports to the chief executive officer with either a direct or indirect reporting relationship to the chair of the board. Governance professionals are required to manage complex workflows, political and high-profile issues, multiple internal and external personalities, and tricky jurisdictional questions (such as which body in the university has the authority to make decisions on a given matter, and what is the appropriate consultation and approval path for a policy document). They are integral to the work of the board and to supporting the board chair.

8) Legal Counsel

In some cases, the role of university secretary is combined with that of chief legal officer (sometimes called "general counsel," although less often than in other sectors). The boards of large and complex organizations such as universities would do well to ensure that they have access to sound legal advice. This is an area in which universities in Canada lag well behind other large and complex organizations. Most universities should have a general counsel because the governance work of the university is complementary to the legal work. In my work, I have always served in the combined role charged with managing governance and legal functions.[13] I think this

---

12 Timothy C Caboni, "Institutional Advancement in Higher Education: Historical Background, Areas of Institutional Advancement," Education Encyclopedia (n.d.), online: State University https://education.stateuniversity.com/pages/2088/Institutional-Advancement-in-Higher-Education.html.
13 Cheryl Foy, "All Universities Should Have a General Counsel," *University Affairs* (29 August 2019), online: University Affairs www.universityaffairs.ca/?s=general+counsel.

structure works well, but other structures can work well, too. The most important thing to ensure is that *both* the governance professional *and* the board have access to legal advice when necessary. Legal counsel can provide invaluable support to the governance professional as legally sensitive and difficult matters regularly arise. To fulfil its fiduciary duties, the board sometimes needs legal advice. In situations where the legal and governance functions are split, other measures should be taken to ensure that the university's senior legal officer has access to the board and vice versa.

9) Other Functions and Executives

A quick survey of the leadership teams of even ten universities across Canada will show you that, while the above roles do not vary greatly, each leadership team is unique. While responsibility for operations sometimes sits with the vice-president of finance and administration/operations, these functions are sometimes served by separate executives. For example, the University of Calgary has a vice-president facilities, as well as a vice-president finance and services. The University of Toronto has a chief financial officer and in addition, a vice-president operations and real estate partnerships & vice-provost, academic operations. Other portfolios sometimes represented at the senior leadership level (reporting to the president) include international (international recruitment of students, relationships with international institutions), equity and inclusion, strategic initiatives, communications, health (usually where there is a medical school), students or student life, institutional planning, and analysis.

This chapter is intended to provide board members with an overview of university administration. It is essential background information. There are also strategic implications arising from the administrative organization structure. Strategic priorities and strategic risks should have ownership at the senior leadership level. If, for example, equity, diversity, and inclusion are strategic priorities, there should be a senior leader with responsibility for this priority. Budget allocated to senior leaders should align with the strategic priorities and strategic risks assigned to the leader. The organization structure should reflect that senior leaders have responsibility for important stakeholders. In conclusion, the administration is an important partner in governance.

CHAPTER 8

Key External Stakeholders: Government

A. KEY EXTERNAL STAKEHOLDERS

Understanding and addressing the interests of all stakeholders is critical to making a contribution and fulfilling your fiduciary duty as a board member. The ecosystem of universities is such that your stakeholders will be multiple and from a wide variety of groups. When making key decisions, the board should ensure it has identified the stakeholders affected and that it understands the effects of the decisions on those stakeholders and their interests. Chapters 8, 9, and 10 are intended to give board members an overview of who the external stakeholders may be.

B. GOVERNMENTS: THE BACKGROUND

Universities have relationships with all levels of government. The Canadian *Constitution Act, 1867* provides that provinces have exclusive authority over education within the province.[1] However, the federal government has long played an active role in education, and the relationships between and among universities and the federal and provincial governments has long been difficult to navigate. David Cameron's description of the challenges of the 1980s gives a glimpse at the foundations of the ongoing tensions and patterns we see today:

---

1   *Constitution Act, 1867* (UK), 30 & 31 Vict, c 3, s 93.

> The 1980s were marked by a continuing search for new directions in public policy.... Provincial policy was characterized by the mostly frustrated pursuit of coordination and rationalization of institutions and programs, doubts about the effectiveness of intermediary agencies, growing interest in and use of targeted funding, and efforts to forge partnerships with industry in harnessing university research more closely to perceived levers of economic development. The federal government was also frustrated in its efforts to influence provincial policy, and moved instead to hold the line on increases in the value of its unconditional grants, while picking up from the provinces a growing interest in university-industry co-operation in research.[2]

It is safe to say that university relationships with federal and provincial governments remain complex. For board members, it is important to understand the attitudes of the governments of the day to universities. These attitudes are the foundation for policy and funding decisions critical to universities. You should also understand your institution's government-relations strategy. And now a few words to expand on university relationships with each level of government.

C. PROVINCIAL GOVERNMENTS

Provincial governments loom large in the lives of universities.

1) University Legislation

Universities are created by and operate under provincial legislation. Some are created by one piece of provincial legislation common to universities in the province, but the majority are created by individual pieces of legislation. Table 8.1 below presents the list of Universities Canada member universities[3] and a subset of the information helpfully amassed in the appendix of *Handbook of Canadian Higher Education Law*. Please note that government ministry names change regularly and the ministries below were current at the time of publication.[4]

---

2 David M Cameron, *More Than an Academic Question: Universities, Government and Public Policy in Canada* (Halifax: The Institute for Research on Public Policy, 1991) at xxvii.
3 "Member Universities," Universities Canada (n.d.), online: Universities Canada www.univcan.ca/universities/member-universities.
4 Theresa Shanahan, Michelle Nilson & Li-Jeen Broshko, *Handbook of Canadian Higher Education Law* (Kingston: School of Policy Studies, Queen's University, 2015) at 301–37.

Table 8.1 Legislation creating Canadian universities

Province	Number of Universities (UC Members)	Provincial or Individual Legislation	Name of Provincial Legislation	Ministry Title (2020)
Alberta	8	Provincial	Post-Secondary Learning Act, SA 2003, c P-19	Ministry of Innovation and Advanced Education
British Columbia	11	Provincial and individual acts	University Act, RSBC 1996, c 468	Ministry of Advanced Education
Manitoba	6	Individual acts	Not applicable	Economic Development and Training
New Brunswick	4	Individual charters or acts	Not applicable	Department of Post-secondary Education, Training and Labour
Newfoundland and Labrador	1 (three campuses)	Individual act	Not applicable	Department of Advanced Education and Skills
Nova Scotia	9	Individual acts	Not applicable	Department of Labour and Advanced Education
Ontario	30	Individual charters or acts of provincial or federal legislature.[5]	Not applicable	Ministry of Colleges and Universities
Prince Edward Island	1	Individual act	Not applicable	Department of Innovation and Advanced Learning
Quebec	20	Individual charters (pre-1968) or acts	Not applicable	Ministry of Higher Education, Research, Science and Technology
Saskatchewan	6	Individual acts	Not applicable	Ministry of Advanced Education

---

[5] "Terms of Reference," Royal Military College of Canada (n.d.), online: Government of Canada www.rmc-cmr.ca/en/college-commandants-office/terms-reference.

Through legislation, the provinces control the power to grant university degrees in the province.[6] One of the trends that will be of interest to governing board members (as it raises existential questions for universities), is the expansion of degree-granting powers to other entities. As Theresa Shanahan et al note:

> [The] distinction by institutional type and degree-granting authority has become blurred over the last two decades as the expansion of higher education in Canada and the expansion of degree-granting status to the non-university post-secondary institutions ... have given rise to a range and diversity of post-secondary institutions, structures, programs, and degree types.... Universities continue to grant degrees, but increasingly colleges and other non-university post-secondary institutions are offering applied and associate degrees.[7]

The expansion of degree-granting powers to more institutions changes the competitive landscape for universities. For boards and university leaders, it also raises strategic questions as to how each university will differentiate its academic offerings within an increasingly competitive educational landscape.

2) Funding

The key way in which provinces involve themselves in universities is through funding. All universities receive operating funding from their provincial governments. The traditional model was to transfer operating funds based on enrolment. Currently, however (and in keeping with the trends described by David Cameron in the 1980s), provincial governments are actively engaged in using funding to ensure that universities act in alignment with government policy. This is a trend that should be of interest to university boards. Another term for it is "performance-based funding." It has the potential to dramatically affect university funding. Ontario is a leader in this area, having developed ten performance measures and set the goal of tying up to 60 percent of operating funds to these measures by 2024.[8]

---

6 See, for example, *Post-secondary Education Choice and Excellence Act, 2000*, SO 2000, c 36, Sch.
7 Shanahan, Nilson & Broshko, above note 4 at 38.
8 Joe Friesen, "New Metrics for Ontario University and College Funding Include Employment and Graduation Rates," *Globe and Mail* (16 April 2019), online: www.theglobeandmail.com/canada/article-new-metrics-for-ontario-university-and-college-funding-include.

Alberta and Manitoba have similar intentions, and Saskatchewan and New Brunswick are considering performance-based funding.

There is significant concern that the traditional autonomy of universities across the country is being reduced "in the face of increasing government regulation and accountability measures."[9] These measures are highly controversial within the university community as members bemoan the loss of independence that is fundamental to their work. In particular, there are concerns among faculty. One scholar states:

> [Performance-based funding] was never about achieving the fundamental missions of the university; it is about budget cuts and control to be exercised by government; it adds another layer of unnecessary bureaucracy to which universities must respond to the detriment of their fundamental mission.[10]

We will continue the discussion about funding in Chapter 16.

3) Board Appointees

Provinces also involve themselves in university board appointments. The legislation that creates universities commonly contains provisions stipulating that the relevant provincial government may appoint one or more members to the board. For example, all of Alberta's eight universities are created by, and subject to, one piece of legislation the *Post-Secondary Learning Act*.[11] The Act provides that university board composition is fixed, and either the minister or the lieutenant governor of the province appoints the chair and all members of the board other than the president and the chancellor.[12] As a further example, in Ontario, many universities have provincial appointees to their boards.[13] These appointments are called Lieutenant Governor in Council appointments (LGICs) and they are made through the Ontario Public

---

9   Julia A Eastman et al, "Provincial Oversight and Institutional Autonomy: Findings of a Comparative Study of Canadian University Governance" (2018) 48 *Canadian Journal of Higher Education* 65 at 78.

10 "The Rise of Performance-Based Funding," Canadian Association of University Teachers (April 2020), online: CAUT www.caut.ca/bulletin/2020/04/rise-performance-based-funding at 4.

11 *Post-Secondary Learning Act*, SA 2003, c P-19.5.

12 *Ibid*, s 16.

13 See for example: Ryerson University (nine LGICs), Ontario Tech University (two LGICs), Laurentian University (five LGICs), Lakehead University (three LGICs), Guelph University (four LGICs), and University of Ottawa (four LGICs).

Appointments Secretariat.[14] There are other examples across the country. If the government acts arbitrarily and without input from the university in its appointment of board members, it can be very difficult for university boards to follow good governance practices in board recruitment, and there are implications for board culture. For example, it is recommended that recruitment be done on the basis of skills matrices with attention paid to diversity.[15] Where governments ignore the internal processes of universities and parachute candidates into board roles, they undermine the integrity of the very boards on which they rely to act in the public interest, and in the university's best interests, through the protection of all university stakeholders.

Provinces are also involved in various ways in attempts at system coordination and quality assurance. This means that provinces are involved in regulating institutions' academic quality control processes.[16] Furthermore, there is daily news about other ways in which provincial governments are involved in the day-to-day lives of universities. For example, on 8 May 2020, the following announcements were made and profiled in the helpful daily Top Ten published by Academica:

> MB announces dollar-for-dollar fund matching, top up to bursary programs
>
> ON presses pause on performance-based funding, AB to introduce policies later this month[17]

Across the country, provincial governments' actions and policies have a significant impact on universities. As a board member, understanding your provincial government's perspective and being familiar with its activity is vital. Under the guidance of your president and executive responsible for government relations, board members can also provide helpful support in the development of positive government relations.

---

14 "Public Appointments," Government of Canada (25 June 2018), online: www.ontario.ca/page/public-appointments.
15 Emma Graney, "'Blindsided': UCP Blasted for Mass Appointments to Boards, Commissions," *Edmonton Journal* (17 August 2019), online: www.edmontonjournal.com/news/politics/ucp-mass-appoints-friends-to-20-public-boards-including-wcb-aglc-and-universities.
16 Universities Canada provides a helpful overview of the quality assurance framework within each province: "Provincial Quality Assurance Systems," Universities Canada (n.d.), online: www.univcan.ca/universities/quality-assurance/provincial-quality-assurance-systems.
17 "Today's Top Ten," Academica Group (15 October 2020), Academica Group Inc, online: www.academica.ca/topten. A subscription is highly recommended for all university board members.

D. FEDERAL GOVERNMENT

The role of the federal government in daily university life is less obvious but still significant. This role has evolved over the years.

1) Operations

The federal government plays an indirect role in funding post-secondary education through transfer payments to the provinces. These payments are provided under a set of terms and conditions. In 1995, the transfer payments were "drastically reduced and significantly restructured ... becoming one block fund known as the Canada Health and Social Transfer (or CHST)." In 2003, this transfer was further restructured and split into a transfer for health care, and another "for postsecondary education, programs for children and social programs."[18] The conditions under which the federal government transfers are made has changed over time, but the net effect has been a decrease in federal transfer amounts going to the post-secondary sector for operations. Shanahan et al note that "[w]hen calculating the decrease in the transfer payments to postsecondary education against the increase in student enrolments between 1994/95 and 2004/05, per student funding in Canadian postsecondary education decreased by almost 50 percent."[19] Although federal transfer payments to provinces in support of post-secondary education have decreased, the federal government remains a crucial stakeholder as it supports university research and is also active in providing student support.

2) Research Funding

A 1972 senate committee paved the way for the future focus of the federal government on the funding of university research by drawing a distinction between the teaching and research functions of a university, allowing "teaching to be equated with education, in its constitutional sense, and therefore a provincial responsibility."[20] This study proposed then that "the Canadian government would assume responsibility for basic research in

---

18   Shanahan, Nilson & Broshko, above note 4 at 26.
19   *Ibid* at 26–27.
20   Cameron, above note 2 at 219.

universities."[21] Today, the federal government is a major sponsor of university research through multiple research-funding vehicles.[22]

3) Student Support

The federal government has long played a significant role in supporting students. Registered education savings programs are permissible as a result of federal legislation: the *Canada Education Savings Act*.[23] The federal government is responsible for the Canada Student Loans Program under which the federal government provides funding (in cooperation with the provinces) in the form of non-repayable grants and repayable loans.[24]

E. MUNICIPAL GOVERNMENT

As large employers, property owners, developers of property, contributors to community development, and entities that both enrich and sometimes create problems for their local communities, local and regional governments are key stakeholders for the university. The relationship is an important one. Issues can arise between universities and local governments over land use and infrastructure costs associated with university development, student behaviour and impact on the local community, university participation in and support for community issues, and many other matters. At the same time, local governments and universities are essential partners in many development and community initiatives, and local governments are often donors to universities, making contributions of money or land, or sharing resources. For universities, local government is a key partner in enhancing the student experience and thus attracting new students.

---

21 *Ibid.*
22 For an overview of the agencies and programs through which the federal government funds university research, see: www.canada.ca/en/research-coordinating-committee.html. For information about the three primary agencies involved in university research, see: www.nserc-crsng.gc.ca/NSERC-CRSNG/Index_eng.asp; https://cihr-irsc.gc.ca/e/193.html; and www.sshrc-crsh.gc.ca.
23 *Canada Education Savings Act*, SC 2004, c 26.
24 "Canada Student Loans and Grants," Government of Canada (n.d.), online: Government of Canada www.canada.ca/en/employment-social-development/programs/canada-student-loans-grants.html.

F. CONCLUSION

This chapter is intended to provide board members with a basic understanding of the roles each level of government plays in university life. The chapter demonstrates that governments at every level are key stakeholders for universities. Provincial legislation creates universities and also creates the legal context within which universities operate. Provincial fiscal policy has a dramatic effect on the financial fortunes of institutions. As governments are key stakeholders for universities, boards must consider the effect of university decisions on the relevant government stakeholder. Further, boards must understand the effect that government policy and regulation have on universities and must govern within those constraints. Understanding your university's government relations strategy is important, as the board may well have a role to play here. Finally, boards should understand the struggle universities face in preserving institutional autonomy in the context of increasing policy and regulation and their financial dependence on government.

CHAPTER 9

Key External Stakeholders: Community

A. INDIGENOUS PEOPLES

Indigenous peoples are key stakeholders for universities, and universities have committed to supporting and advancing the interests of Indigenous peoples. For some universities, the relationship and commitment to Indigenous peoples will be more obvious because there will be a specific mandate in the institution's act or bylaws to serve First Nations communities. There may be designated board seats for First Nations community members.[1] In the preamble to the *First Nations University of Canada Act*, it is provided that

> the Saskatchewan Indian Federated College, now the First Nations University of Canada, was established in 1976 under the authority of Saskatchewan First Nations, as an academically integrated and independently administered institution to serve the academic, cultural and spiritual needs of First Nations and society in general.[2]

---

1   "Governance and Human Resources Committee Terms of Reference," First Nations University of Canada (29 July 2020), online: www.fnuniv.ca/governance. Also, Algoma University and Lakehead University have designated board seats for First Nations.
2   *First Nations University of Canada Act, 2010*, online: Federation of Saskatchewan Indian Nations www.fnuniv.ca/wp-content/uploads/2010_June_10_-_FN_University_of_Canada_Act_-_Amended.pdf at 1.

As a further example, bylaw 7.2 of Algoma University states that it is part of the university's mission to "cultivate cross-cultural learning between aboriginal communities and other communities, in keeping with the history of Algoma University College and its geographic site." The same bylaws go on to provide that "[a] minimum of four Board members shall be appointed as representatives of Anishinaabe organizations and/or communities."[3] Board members should be sure to understand how and if your institution's constituting documents enshrine a commitment to Indigenous peoples.

While many institutions do not have an enshrined commitment to a relationship with Indigenous peoples in their acts or bylaws, the Truth and Reconciliation Commission of Canada's *Calls to Action* report has many implications for the post-secondary sector and many universities have made commitments to advancing truth and reconciliation through a process of indigenizing their universities.[4] Indigenization takes many forms, and as a board member you need to be educated about, aware of, and supportive of your university's plans to address the recommendations and to participate in truth and reconciliation. Understanding that the sector has made a commitment to advancing truth and reconciliation and indigenization also means that your board should ensure that your university is meeting its commitments in this regard. The list of actions that universities are called upon to undertake is reproduced in Appendix 9.1 below.

B. DONORS

Donations to universities are a crucial source of funding for university initiatives. Board members have a significant role to play in supporting the fundraising activities of a university, and board members themselves may be asked to donate, facilitate, or advocate for donations to the university. There are boards on which all members are expected to donate. There may be expectations to host fundraising events or make introductions to potential donors in your network. Not all board members are comfortable with this role. Some feel that donating their time to the governance of the university is sufficient. Others are comfortable supporting the university in this

---

3   Algoma University, By-Laws No. 7.2, I b and III 3 (20 June 2016), online: www.algomau.ca/wp-content/uploads/2018/11/Algoma-University-By-laws-Version-7.2.pdf.

4   "Advancing Reconciliation Through Higher Education: 2017 Survey Findings," Universities Canada (April 2018), online: Universities Canada www.univcan.ca/wp-content/uploads/2018/10/Indigenous_survey_findings_2017_factsheet_25Apr_.pdf.

way. Coming to an early understanding about what is expected, and being clear about what you can and will bring as a board member is important. If you can help the university raise money in any way, it will be appreciated.

One of the key issues about which board members should be aware is the potential for donor interference with university autonomy. As your advancement professionals will tell you, the donor of today seeks more involvement and control, and is more interested in clarity about the use of donated funds. In 2012, an article in *The Globe and Mail* summarized it nicely:

> The deals struck today are often more complex, the donors less passive, and some schools have landed in hot water in their eagerness to do new things, and to keep benefactors from taking their precious dollars elsewhere.[5]

It is important that when funding research, donors or donations do not interfere with faculty independence or academic freedom. To put it simply, donors may give money to a research project, but they cannot control the project, for if they do, they are interfering with university autonomy, research integrity, and potentially with the academic freedom of faculty involved in the project. For example, Carleton University was forced to rewrite an agreement with a donor who had negotiated control over hiring decisions.[6] In late 2015, the University of Calgary faced criticism about its relationship with Enbridge, a major donor. The university retained a former judge (McMahon J) to review the university's relationship with Enbridge. While McMahon J found no wrongdoing, the matter did not end there. The Canadian Association of University Teachers conducted its own investigation and issued a report in late 2017 with very different findings, highly critical of the University of Calgary.[7]

The reputational risks of accepting donations from particular donors must be assessed, and boards must sometimes make decisions not to accept donations or to disengage from donors with whom an affiliation may bring

---

5   James Bradshaw, "The Tricky Business of Funding a University," *Globe and Mail* (17 October 2012), online: www.theglobeandmail.com/news/national/time-to-lead/the-tricky-business-of-funding-a-university/article4619883.
6   *Ibid.*
7   Lisa Keller, "Enbridge Inquiry: University of Calgary President was "clearly" in conflict-of-interest," Canadian Association of University Teachers (11 October 2017), online: CAUT www.caut.ca/latest/2017/10/enbridge-inquiry-university-calgary-president-was-clearly-conflict-interest.

the university into disrepute. For example, Brown University in the United States, faced criticism for accepting donations from a donor whose company had manufactured tear gas. In response, the university amended its gift acceptance policy to make it clear that in accepting a gift, it wasn't endorsing the activities of the donor.[8] In an age of activism, attempts to distance from donors will likely be unsuccessful. A board needs to ensure that its university has clearly articulated its position and risk tolerance in relation to gifts, has a vetting process for accepting gifts, and stays abreast of potential issues.

While not all donor agreements will come to a board of governors for approval, some will, and prior to approving them, boards should satisfy themselves of the propriety of the agreement terms. More generally, board members should be aware of the pressure faced by universities as they navigate the preservation of autonomy and academic freedom, and the expectations of donors to whom these concepts may be foreign. Board members should ensure that there are rigorous contract-management and robust conflict-of-interest practices, and that advancement professionals fully comprehend the need to protect university autonomy and faculty freedoms.

C. PARTNERS: INSTITUTIONS AND INDUSTRY

Another marvellous thing about the university sector is the extent to which collaboration abounds. Faculties collaborate among themselves. They collaborate with those of other universities in Canada and around the world. Universities collaborate. There is collaboration between universities and hospitals, universities and school boards, and universities and government agencies. There is collaboration between universities and a variety of industry partners. From a board perspective, it is important to understand key university partnerships, the university's partnership strategies and priorities, important sectors, and key partner representatives. If the board doesn't understand the university's partnerships or its partnership strategy, the board is unable to consider how board decisions affect this group of stakeholders.

---

8   James Piereson & Naomi S Riley, "Donors Beware: Universities and Museums Find It Harder and Harder to Accept Financial Gifts That Don't Set Off Political Controversy," *City Journal* (19 November 2019), online: Manhattan Institute for Policy Research www.city-journal.org/donors-political-controversy.

D. THE COMMUNITY

The communities in which your institution resides are also stakeholders. A mandate to serve your local community or region may be enshrined in your legislation.[9] Just as students are not a monolithic group, the communities in which universities are situated are made up of groups of university stakeholders. Boards should pay attention to these "town-gown" relationships. An excellent article by Jennifer Massey et al makes the following point:

> Town–gown relations are a pressing priority for city governments and university administrations. For city governments, universities hold a key to economic development (Mullin & Kotval, 2012). For universities, partnerships with the local community are politically important. In Ontario, the call for universities to demonstrate their "regional relevance," and discussion about the benefits of greater differentiation within Ontario's university sector (Weingarten & Deller, 2010), have pressured institutions to demonstrate how they support the local community and economy. One of the most common measures of this impact is the proportion of university students who remain in the local area after graduation. In the new knowledge-based economy, or what Florida (2002) termed the "creative economy," university graduates are the cornerstone of local economic development strategies.[10]

Board members should pay attention to the contribution their university makes to the region. This contribution should be articulated and reinforced. The goal should be to ensure that the town, city, and region within which the university is situated understands the value of the university to the community, and most importantly, supports the university.

As well as the interests (which might be mostly economic) of the town, city, or region in which the university is situated, however, there are those of many stakeholder groups. The local rape crisis centre may have an interest in initiatives to address sexual violence on your campus. The local historical society may have an interest in campus buildings. Those with a passion for

---

9   *University of Ontario Institute of Technology Act, 2002*, RSO 2002, c 8, online: www.ontario.ca/laws/statute/02u08. This Act provides that one of the objects of the university is to contribute to the advancement of Ontario in the Canadian and global contexts, with particular focus on the Durham region and Northumberland County.

10 Jennifer Massey, Sean Field & Yolande Chan, "Partnering for Economic Development: How Town-Gown Relations Impact Local Economic Development in Small and Medium Cities" (2014) 44 *Canadian Journal of Higher Education* 152 at 153–54.

horses may be very interested in the fact that your lands are home to the grave of famous racehorse, Northern Dancer, and may be concerned in the university's efforts to preserve the grave.[11] Boards should understand and appreciate the scope of the community within which the university is located, the nature and state of the relationship between them, and measures taken to improve town-gown relations.

E. CONCLUSION

This chapter does not present an exhaustive list of community stakeholders for your university, but it's a list that should get you started. As a university board, there is value in an expansive and thoughtful approach to stakeholders. Stakeholders evolve. As you consider community stakeholders, appreciate that there is a present state and a future state. How is your community changing and where is it heading? What will it look like in the future and how does any change you anticipate affect the university? It's valuable to consider the impact of decisions on these stakeholders of the future or, as I've heard them described, "moral stakeholders."[12]

---

11 "Northern Dancer: Little Horse, Big Legacy" *Oshawa Express* (18 April 2018), online: www.oshawaexpress.ca/northern-dancer-little-horse-big-legacy.
12 Attributed to Jeff Leclerc, University Secretary, University of Manitoba.

APPENDIX 9.1
Truth and Reconciliation Commission: Calls to Action

1) Ensure institutional commitment at every level to develop opportunities for Indigenous students.
2) Be student-centred: focus on the learners, learning outcomes, and learning abilities, and create opportunities that promote student success.
3) Recognize the importance of indigenization of curricula through responsive academic programming, support programs, orientations, and pedagogies.
4) Recognize the importance of Indigenous education leadership through representation at the governance level and within faculty, professional, and administrative staff.
5) Continue to build welcoming and respectful learning environments on campuses through the implementation of academic programs, services, support mechanisms, and spaces dedicated to Indigenous students.
6) Continue to develop resources, spaces, and approaches that promote dialogue between Indigenous and non-Indigenous students.
7) Continue to develop accessible learning environments off-campus.
8) Recognize the value of promoting partnerships among educational and local Indigenous communities and continue to maintain a collaborative and consultative process on the specific needs of Indigenous students.
9) Build on successful experiences and initiatives already in place at universities across the country to share and learn from promising practices, while recognizing the differences in jurisdictional and institutional mission.
10) Recognize the importance of sharing information within the institution, and beyond, to inform current and prospective Indigenous students of the array of services, programs, and supports available to them on campus.
11) Recognize the importance of providing greater exposure and knowledge for non-Indigenous students on the realities, histories, cultures, and beliefs of Indigenous people in Canada.
12) Recognize the importance of fostering intercultural engagement among Indigenous and non-Indigenous students, faculty, and staff.
13) Recognize the role of institutions in creating an enabling and supportive environment for a successful and high-quality K-12 experience for Aboriginal youth.[13]

---

13 "Universities Canada Principles on Indigenous Education" Universities Canada (29 June 2015), online: Universities Canada www.univcan.ca/media-room/media-releases/universities-canada-principles-on-Indigenous-education.

CHAPTER 10

Key External Stakeholders: Groups and Associations

A. TYPES OF GROUPS AND ASSOCIATIONS

The university ecosystem is complex. The purpose of this chapter is to give the board member a sense of the type and nature of other groups and organizations within this ecosystem. These entities have been described as "a vital piece of the post-secondary governance structure."[1] Because there are too many organizations to enumerate individually, they have been grouped and described in the following categories of associations: (1) academic, (2) faculty, (3) administrative, (4) student, (5) athletic.

1) Academic Associations

This is a broad category[2] that includes Universities Canada (described below) and many others. As one example, you will hear reference to a group of fifteen Canadian research universities calling itself simply the "U15." This group describes itself as "a collective of some of Canada's most

---

1 David Young & Wendy Kraglund-Gauthier, "Governance and Administration of Postsecondary Education Associations: A Vital Piece of the Postsecondary Governance Structure" in Theresa Shanahan, Michelle Nilson & Li-Jeen Broshko, *Handbook of Canadian Higher Education Law* (Kingston: School of Policy Studies, Queen's University, 2015) at 113.
2 For a longer description of these groups, see *ibid*.

research-intensive universities."[3] As another example, Ontario universities have formed an association called the Council of Ontario Universities.[4]

2) Faculty Associations

As discussed in Chapter 6, most, but not all, faculty are members of a faculty association bargaining unit. Many faculty associations belong to the Canadian Association of University Teachers (CAUT). CAUT is the national association of faculty associations and is described more fully below.

3) Administrative Associations

University administrators are connected through formal and informal inter- and intra-provincial and national groups too numerous to mention. By way of example, there is the Canadian Association of University Business Officers (CAUBO), a group established in 1937 to "[represent] chief administrative and [chief] financial officers at over 100 universities and affiliated colleges" to enable "excellence in higher education administration."[5] CAUBO very helpfully provides an annual report containing detailed financial information for universities and colleges across the country.[6] Another example is the Canadian Association of University Solicitors, a group of lawyers that work both in-house and as external counsel providing legal support to Canadian universities. This group describes itself as follows:

> The Canadian Association of University Solicitors (CAUS) is a nebulous and mysterious group of friends and colleagues who, since 1978, have worked to support universities across Canada through the provision of quality legal services.[7]

At the board level, there is an organization known as CUBA (the Canadian University Boards Association) through which university governance

---

3 "Group of Canadian Research Universities," U15 (n.d.), online: U15 www.u15.ca.
4 "Council of Ontario Universities," COU (n.d.), online: COU www.cou.ca.
5 "About CAUBO," Canadian Association of University Business Officers (n.d.), online: CAUBO www.caubo.ca/discover-caubo/about-caubo.
6 "Financial Information of Universities and Degree-Granting Colleges, 2017/2018," Statistics Canada Catalogue no. 11-001-X (24 July 2019), online: Statistics Canada www150.statcan.gc.ca/n1/daily-quotidien/190724/dq190724a-eng.pdf at 1.
7 "Canadian Association of University Solicitors," CAUS (n.d.), online: CAUS www.caous.wildapricot.org.

professionals and board leaders connect through list services and an annual governance conference.[8] If you hear your board secretary and board chair laughingly advise that they are off to CUBA, now you'll be in on the joke. There are many other examples of administrative associations that enable universities to share experiences, knowledge, policies, and best practices. These associations are very active.

4) Student Associations

Most universities have a student association on campus and there may be more than one association. A common split is between undergraduate and graduate student associations. Providing the infrastructure and funding for student clubs is a key role for student associations, as well as providing support services. For example, student health plans are often offered through a campus student association. Student associations can be important partners in supporting students and enhancing the student experience. As described more fully below, these associations are typically financed through student fees collected by the university and transferred to the association. (This money is a subset of the ancillary fees that universities collect for a variety of services.) A number of universities have experienced conflict with their student associations, sometimes over the management of the fees passed on to the student association.[9] Student associations also experience conflict with their members.[10] In both cases, there is potential for negative consequences for your university's student life and for your university's reputation. On a national and provincial level, student associations are affiliated. More detail is provided on these national groups below.

5) Athletic Associations

Canadian university and college sport is governed by national and regional associations. The national body was for many years called CIS (Canadian Interuniversity Sport), but in 2016 was rebranded as U Sports. Varsity athletics are a key part of campus culture. Organizations like U Sports and their provincial and regional counterparts require that their members adhere to a

---

8 "CUBA 2020 AGM," Canadian University Boards Association (n.d.), online: CUBA www.cuba-accau.ca/Home.
9 *Ryerson Students' Union v Ryerson University*, 2020 ONSC 1490.
10 *Naggar v The Student Association at Durham College and UOIT*, 2018 ONSC 1247.

set of compliance obligations and principles. These compliance rules apply to matters ranging from the hosting of national championships to rules relating to scholarships for students athletes.[11]

B. AN INTRODUCTION TO SOME NATIONAL UNIVERSITY ASSOCIATIONS

The associations discussed below are national in scope and thus likely of relevance to board members across the country.

1) Universities Canada

Formerly known as the Association of Universities and Colleges of Canada and established in 1911, Universities Canada (UC) describes itself as the "voice of Canadian universities." It is a non-governmental, member-based organization counting approximately ninety-five institutions as members. UC does the following:

- Advocate[s] for Canadian universities at the federal level
- Provide[s] a forum for university leaders to share ideas and address challenges in higher education
- Support[s] students by providing online information on university study and offering scholarships on behalf of private-sector companies
- Foster[s] collaboration among universities and governments, the private sector, communities and international partners to help build a better world[12]

UC is managed by its president. The president serves on the UC board along with the presidents of twelve member institutions. UC's current areas of policy focus include:

- copyright and fair dealing
- social impact
- Indigenous education
- global experience
- equity, diversity, and inclusion

---

11 "U Sports," U Sports (n.d.), online: www.usports.ca/en.
12 "About Us," Universities Canada (n.d.), online: Universities Canada www.univcan.ca/about-us.

- research and innovation
- skills and talent[13]

UC provides tremendous resources for its members via its website and its magazine *University Affairs*, and UC facilitates a great deal of knowledge sharing and cooperation among its members.

2) Canadian Association of University Teachers

Canadian Association of University Teachers (CAUT) was founded in 1951 and describes itself as "the national voice for academic staff representing 72,000 teachers, librarians, researchers, general staff and other academic professionals at some 125 universities and colleges[14] across the country."[15] CAUT engages in the following activities on behalf of its members:

- lobbying government
- providing collective bargaining support
- providing legal support
- providing conferences and training
- investigating threats to academic freedom
- engaging in research
- publishing various documents, including a monthly publication[16]

A quick review of the CAUT website sees them opining on a variety of matters, including:

- supporting the federal government's initiative to provide ten days of paid sick leave
- remote teaching during the COVID-19 pandemic
- return-to-work planning during the COVID-19 pandemic, with particular attention to the role of faculty associations and joint health and safety committees
- guidelines for reopening campus in the COVID-19 context

---

13 "Priorities," Universities Canada (n.d.), online: Universities Canada www.univcan.ca/priorities.
14 "Member Associations," Canadian Association of University Teachers (n.d.), online: CAUT www.caut.ca/about-us/members-locals.
15 "About Us," Canadian Association of University Teachers (n.d.), online: CAUT www.caut.ca/about-us.
16 Ibid.

- permanently discontinuing performance-based provincial funding plans
- the Federal Court of Appeal case between York University and Access Copyright[17]

CAUT is an active defender of academic freedom and it advocates for a very broad definition thereof. Where CAUT concludes that a university is engaged in behaviour or practices that undermine academic freedom (as defined by CAUT), it does not hesitate to take the institution to task. CAUT is also interested in the governance of universities. It is a promoter of shared governance and believes that such governance is "under attack":

> University ... boards are increasingly controlled by corporate appointees with little understanding of important academic matters. Decision-making powers are concentrated in the hands of a few—who act behind closed doors—while the voices of academic staff and other key stakeholders are being weakened or silenced.[18]

CAUT is one of more than ten national and provincial collective associations in Canada.[19] It is valuable for board members to understand the perspective of these collective associations. It is also valuable for board members to understand the extent to which the associations reflect the views of faculty on your particular campus. This will vary from issue to issue and from campus to campus. The board should be aware that while associations do not speak for all academics, they have significant influence on their member associations and the issues on which they focus.

---

17   There is ongoing litigation between York University and Access Copyright. The Supreme Court of Canada recently granted leave to appeal the Federal Court of Appeal decision to both York University and Access Copyright, and the matter will be heard by the SCC in 2021. A summary of the Federal Court of Appeal decision and its implications can be found here: www.fasken.com/en/knowledge/2020/06/2-york-university-v-access-copyright-decision.

18   "Shared Governance. Quality Education," Canadian Association of University Teachers (n.d.), online: CAUT www.caut.ca/campaigns/shared-governance

19   There are also: National Union of the Canadian Association of University Teachers, Ontario Confederation of University Faculty Associations, Confederation of University Faculty Associations of BC, Federation of Post-Secondary Educators of BC, Confederation of Alberta Faculty Associations, Alberta Colleges and Institutes Faculties Association, Manitoba Organization of Faculty Associations, Fédération québécoise des professeures et professeurs d'université, Fédération nationale des enseignantes et des enseignants du Québec (representing CEGEP Unions), Federation of New Brunswick Faculty Associations, and the Association of Nova Scotia University Teachers.

3) Canadian Federation of Students and Canadian Alliance of Student Associations

Canadian Federation of Students (CFS) describes itself as a "student movement." It represents approximately 500,000 students at sixty-four institutions across Canada.[20] Canadian Alliance of Student Associations (CASA) is a similar but smaller group that is partnered with the Quebec Student Union and counts twenty-three institutions as members. CASA indicates that its members represent some 344,000 students.[21] A note of caution to boards and others regarding the membership counts for these associations. These national associations count student associations as their members. When students go to a university, it is typically mandatory for them to pay fees to support and join the university's student association. Membership is a default and not an active choice. Based on my experience, the level of student engagement in student association governance is very low and a tiny fraction of students vote for the leaders of their association. I am a strong proponent of active engagement between the board and its key student stakeholder group, but boards should understand the level of engagement of the students with their association, and should not rely only on the student association as the sole voice of students.

C. RANKINGS ENTITIES

I will include here only a brief word about rankings entities. Boards should be aware that there are various mechanisms by which universities are ranked. Each rankings organization uses different methodologies and focuses on different attributes and metrics. You will be aware that *Maclean's* annually publishes a magazine dedicated to ranking Canadian universities in fourteen categories.[22] The National Survey of Student Engagement Results, like the *Maclean's* ranking information, is another set of data about which the board should be aware. There are also global ranking entities such as QS World University Rankings, THE World University Rankings,

---

20   "Canadian Federation of Students," CFS (n.d.), online: www.cfs-fcee.ca.
21   "Members," Canadian Alliance of Student Associations (n.d.), online: CASA www.casa-acae.com/members. CASA has twenty-three institutional members who represent 264,000 students.
22   For example, in 2020, the rankings were published in "University Rankings 2020," *Maclean's* (3 October 2019). The methodology for 2020 is included here: Mary Dwyer, "Maclean's University Rankings 2020: Our Methodology," *Maclean's* (3 October 2019).

and Academic Ranking of World Universities, among others.[23] Fewer than ten Canadian universities are included in the top 200 schools. The value of the rankings is debated.[24] Again, however, you should be aware of your university's standing as a point of information.

D. CONCLUSION

This chapter is intended to give board members a sense of the ecosystem of groups and associations that have formed within the post-secondary sector. These groups and associations all play roles — either in regulating an aspect of university life, in collecting and giving a provincial or national voice to interests and perspectives of groups working inside the university, in enabling collaboration and the benefit of shared experience, or, as in the case of the rankings entities, passing judgment on university activities. Just having a sense of these players either as compliance bodies, critics, or sources of information and support is important to a board member's appreciation of the complex world within which universities operate.

---

23 See, for example: "National Survey of Student Engagement Results," Indiana University Bloomington School of Education (n.d.), online: https://nsse.indiana.edu/research/annual-results; "QS World University Rankings," Quacquarelli Symonds (n.d.), online: QS www.qs.com; "THE World University Rankings," Times Higher Education (n.d.), online: THE www.timeshighereducation.com/world-university-rankings/2021/world-ranking#!; "Academic Ranking of World Universities," Shanghai Ranking Consultancy (n.d.), online: ARWU www.shanghairanking.com.

24 Alex Usher, "2020 Rankings Round-Up," Higher Education Strategy Associates (8 September 2020), online: Higher Education Strategy Associates www.higheredstrategy.com/2020-rankings-round-up.

CHAPTER 11

Unique and Essential Concepts

This book is intended to help new governors and those new to working in university governance understand universities and university culture. As such, it has to tackle some of the key concepts essential to understanding the sector. Several of these concepts are intertwined and interdependent. Board members should understand these concepts because they are central to the board's ability to serve as stewards of their universities, central to the board's ability to advance the mission of their institution, and central to ensuring that universities fulfil their important roles in society.

A. ALL THINGS "ACADEMIC"

Board members will hear the words "academic," "academy," "academe," and "academia" used regularly. Merriam-Webster shares the following fascinating information about the root of these words: "Our word academy comes from the Greek word *Akademeia*, the name of the park or grove outside of ancient Athens where the philosopher Plato taught his students."[1]

"Academic" will be used both as an adjective and as a noun. As an adjective, it can be used to describe those matters falling within the purview of a university's academic council or senate. As a noun, it describes those engaged

---

1 Merriam-Webster Online Dictionary: www.merriam-webster.com/dictionary/academy#note-1.

in the scholarly activities of teaching and research at the university. "Academe" is defined as "the part of society, especially universities, that is connected with study and thinking"[2] and "academia" has a similar definition but also includes "the activity or job of studying,"[3] as in "working in academia."

B. UNIVERSITIES AS A "COMMONS"

In his books, Peter MacKinnon talks about universities as a "commons" or a site for debate, discussion, and collaboration. Many universities use this concept to describe virtual or physical places they create to support learning. MacKinnon describes the commons as an ideal, and his description conveys the importance and scope of the space that universities create for the advancement of knowledge:

> A platform or space for the debate, discussion, and collaboration that are both inherent in and essential to the idea of the university. This space is multidimensional and has varying degrees of formality. It is to be found in the governance framework and networks; in campus assemblies, associations and clubs; in classrooms and boardrooms, and common rooms; in myriad gatherings of university communities and individuals on and off campus; and in the social media. Its dimensions are physical and hyper-physical, and it is pervasive.[4]

Board members will encounter the concept of commons in various ways in the university setting. In fact, the commons is what is at the heart of a university, and board members will do well to remember that this is what they are protecting and preserving.

C. INSTITUTIONAL AUTONOMY

Preserving institutional autonomy is an important role for the board and it's not an easy undertaking. When we talk about institutional autonomy, we mean institutional freedom from political and partisan control. In the early 1900s, "provincial governments in Ontario were excessively

---

2   "Academe," *Cambridge Dictionary* (n.d.), online: Cambridge University Press www.dictionary.cambridge.org/dictionary/english/academe?q=Academe.
3   "Academia," *Cambridge Dictionary* (n.d.), online Cambridge University Press www.dictionary.cambridge.org/dictionary/english/academia.
4   Peter MacKinnon, *University Commons Divided: Exploring Debate & Dissent on Campus* (Toronto: University of Toronto Press, 2018) at 4.

and directly involved with the operations of the University of Toronto, even to the extent of political involvement in faculty appointments."[5] This gave rise to a royal commission formed in 1906 (the Flavelle Commission), which reinforced the importance of institutional autonomy for universities.[6] Although in receipt of public funds, universities in Canada are "generally not considered arms of government, they are not state universities and they are not state-controlled."[7] Universities are generally created by their own statutes, charters, or proclamations and operate as independent, not-for-profit corporate entities.[8] A commitment to retaining university independence and autonomy should infuse and inform board decisions.

Models of state-university relations vary from country to country,[9] and Canadian universities have enjoyed a higher degree of autonomy than many.[10] This autonomy is, however, eroding, and universities are experiencing greater provincial government control.[11] Universities created by their own legislation generally experience more independence than those created under a common act (such as those in Western Canada).[12] As Julia Eastman et al note:

> The traditionally high level of institutional autonomy associated with Anglo-American systems appears to be declining in the face of increasing government regulation and accountability measures, and the findings of our study confirm that provincial systems in Canada are following a

---

5   Brent Davis, "Governance and Administration of Post-Secondary Institutions in Canada" in Theresa Shanahan, Michelle Nilson & Li-Jeen Broshko, *Handbook of Canadian Higher Education Law* (Kingston: School of Policy Studies, Queen's University, 2015) at 57.

6   David M Cameron, *More Than an Academic Question: Universities, Government and Public Policy in Canada* (Halifax: The Institute for Research on Public Policy, 1991) at 28. The Flavelle Commission of 1906 saw the dangers of political partisan interference in university governance and instead advised that "[t]he powers of the Crown in respect to the control and management of the University [of Toronto] should be vested in the Board of Governors, chosen by the Lieutenant Governor in Council."

7   Theresa Shanahan, Michelle Nilson & Li-Jeen Broshko, *Handbook of Canadian Higher Education Law* (Kingston: School of Policy Studies, Queen's University, 2015) at 41.

8   Ibid.

9   Ian Austin & Glen A Jones, *Governance of Higher Education: Global Perspectives, Theories and Practices* (New York: Routledge, 2016) at 77.

10 Andrew M Boggs, "Ontario's Royal Commission on the University of Toronto, 1905-06: Political and Historical Factors that Influenced the Final Report of the Flavelle Commission," MA Thesis (2007), online: University of Toronto https://tspace.library.utoronto.ca/handle/1807/65526 at 4.

11 Julia A Eastman et al, "Provincial Oversight and Institutional Autonomy: Findings of a Comparative Study of Canadian University Governance" (2018) 48 *Canadian Journal of Higher Education* 65 at 66.

12 Ibid at 76.

similar trend. Every university in our study was experiencing increased requirements for accountability, and increasing pressures to respond to government priorities.[13]

Boards must understand the importance of institutional autonomy and bring this understanding to governing. In strategy and risk planning, boards must work to understand the forces that are increasingly constraining university independence so that they can work to minimize the effects of these constraints, and so that they can work collectively with other institutions to combat these trends in our society. Boards must ensure effective governance, as it is a cornerstone of institutional autonomy.

Faculty associations are sensitive to the erosion of institutional independence. In 2018, the Ontario provincial government required universities to establish free-speech policies based on a government-specified format. In fact, the universities were threatened with a loss of funding if they failed to adopt free-speech policies.[14] The Canadian Association of University Teachers (CAUT) raised concerns about this requirement, on the basis that it was a threat to institutional autonomy and independence from government. They made the point that institutional independence is fundamental to the ability of an institution to operate. Its executive director is quoted as saying:

> [U]niversities and colleges should set their own policies, not politicians. Institutional autonomy—including the freedom from government diktat—is itself necessary to protect free expression and academic freedom.[15]

As this quotation reveals, although faculty associations share university concerns about the loss of university autonomy, faculty focus is less on the broader implications for universities. Instead, the focus is on the implications of diminished institutional autonomy for faculty freedoms.

The erosion of institutional autonomy is an existential threat to universities and the unique role they play in our society, and boards must consider the implications of university responses to government policy and actions. The response to government action must be strategic, and balance

---

13   *Ibid* at 78.
14   Justin Giovannetti, "Doug Ford Says Ontario Postsecondary Schools Will Require Free-Speech Policies," *Globe and Mail* (30 August 2018), online: www.theglobeandmail.com/canada/article-doug-ford-says-ontario-postsecondary-schools-will-require-free-speech.
15   "Ontario 'Free Speech' Requirements for Universities and Colleges Cause for Concern," Canadian Association of University Teachers (31 August 2018), online: CAUT www.caut.ca/latest/2018/08/ontario-free-speech-requirements-universities-and-colleges-cause-concern.

the demands of the government stakeholder, those of other stakeholders, and institutional independence and self-governance.

D. COLLEGIALITY

The *Cambridge Dictionary* provides two definitions of collegial: (1) "relating to a friendly relationship between colleagues," and (2) "used to describe a method of working in which responsibility is shared among several people."[16] In this book, the focus is on the second type of collegiality — the method of working together in which responsibility is shared. As with other concepts this book reviews, the concept of collegiality is misunderstood even within the university sector. Its meaning is also the subject of debate, and as a board member, you will encounter many opinions about what is and isn't "collegial" or consistent with "collegial practice." Austin and Jones say this about collegiality:

> Collegiality has been the bedrock of university governance practice for centuries and has been touted as the vehicle of institutional effectiveness in the academy. It is a tradition that revolves around conferring, collaborating, and gaining consensus. It is also a collective process for decision-making in which academics play an integral role.[17]

The Austin and Jones quotation helps us understand some of the expectations facing boards. Collegiality demands the following:

- conferring or discussing topics
- collaborating or working together
- preferring consensus-based decision-making processes
- consultation with academics, the academic governing body (as appropriate), and with other university stakeholders

External board members coming from a corporate environment may struggle with the complex and consultative processes that are the necessary foundation for many decisions based on collegiality. Remember, however, that the university community is large and multi-faceted. The importance of conferring, collaborating, achieving as much consensus as possible, and of consulting to secure acceptance and adoption of board or management decisions, cannot be understated.

---

16 "Collegial," *Cambridge Dictionary* (n.d.), online: Cambridge University Press www.dictionary.cambridge.org/dictionary/english/collegial.
17 Austin & Jones, above note 9 at 125.

E. GOVERNANCE: BICAMERAL AND OTHER MODELS

Bicameral governance is a form of governance in which decision-making is divided between two bodies within a university. Very simply, the board is charged with deciding business and administrative matters, while the senate or academic council is charged with responsibility for academic matters. These spheres of decision-making may be complemented by obligations to consult between the two bodies.

Principles of bicameral governance are at the foundation of the criteria for membership in Universities Canada. Among other requirements, a university must be able to demonstrate that it has a governance structure and processes, and an administrative structure appropriate to a university, including:

- authority vested in academic staff for decisions affecting academic programs, including admissions, content, graduation requirements/standards, and related policies and procedures through membership on an elected academic senate or other appropriate elected body representative of academic staff; and
- an independent board of governors, or appropriate equivalent, that:
  » is committed to public accountability and functions in an open and transparent manner;
  » has control over the institution's finances, administration, and appointments;
  » includes appropriate representation from the institution's external stakeholders (including the general public), from academic staff, from students, and from alumni; and
  » uses the institution's resources to advance its mission and goals.

The form of governance under which your university operates is established by provincial statute, and as a board member you should be familiar with the statute that created your institution. Most universities in Canada are bicameral in nature.[18] The University of Toronto is a notable and rare example of unicameral governance.[19] The University of Saskatchewan is

---

18   Moira MacDonald, "University Boards in the Spotlight," *University Affairs* (3 January 2018), online: University Affairs www.universityaffairs.ca/features/feature-article/university-boards-spotlight.

19   Cameron, above note 6 at 329. Cameron describes how the University of Toronto became unicameral at 330 of his book, noting that at the end of the process "[c]ritics of the new structure bemoaned the loss of faculty control. One of the harshest critics was

an example of tricameral governance (a Board of Governors, Senate, and University Council).[20] Whatever the form of governance adopted by your university's statute, it is incumbent upon board members to understand the roles of decision-making bodies within the governing structure. The staff in your institutional secretariat will be invaluable in this regard.

To understand bicameral governance, it helps to know a little history. The Flavelle Commission of 1906 was crucial in shaping university governance in Canada. The commission provided a "framework for bicameralism" and established that there would be two governing bodies within universities. The board would be responsible for administrative matters and for reflecting the "public interest" in university decision-making processes. The senate (made up largely of academic members) would assume responsibility for academic matters. As Peter MacKinnon notes, "Bicameralism can therefore be seen as an attempt to balance public and academic interests within the formal, corporate governance structures of the university."[21] It is important that those involved in governance at universities remember that this balancing of public interests with academic interests is at the heart of the bicameral governance model.

It won't surprise you to know that bicameral governance (such topics as its sufficiency, the university's commitment and adherence to it, the efficacy of senates, etc.) is regularly studied, written about, and debated in the university context. It is incumbent on the board to focus on and advance good and effective governance at your institution. This includes working to promote engagement and good decision-making and to invigorate whatever form of governance model is applicable to your institution.

F. BICAMERAL GOVERNANCE AND UNIONIZATION

Faculty unionization adds significant complexity to governing an entity that has a bicameral system of management. In Peter MacKinnon's opinion, unionization "encroaches on governance and collegial management

---

Murray Ross, former vice-president of University of Toronto and former president of York University. The academic staff seem to have exchanged their virtual control of the academic programme for 12 seats on a 50-man council. On the surface it appears not to be a very good bargain."

20   "University Secretary," University of Saskatchewan (n.d.), online: www.secretariat.usask.ca.
21   MacKinnon, above note 4 at 106. It is important for a university board to understand that in the absence of a board to oversee the university, this role would likely fall to the provincial government. Universities would then lose a significant degree of autonomy.

and challenges their authority."[22] As you gain experience on a university board, you will begin to appreciate the dynamic that Peter MacKinnon is describing. Universities have created governance bodies to serve their institutions and represent the two houses within the university. Faculty associations and collective associations such as CAUT are very focused on inserting themselves into university governance and assuming the role of the academic governance body. While members of senates don't (subject to obligations imposed by governing legislation) technically have fiduciary duties at common law, their role is to act in the best interests of the university as they make decisions. The role is akin to that of a fiduciary and they are supposed to put aside individual stakeholder interests and consider the university as a whole. Members of the academic community complain that their senates are ineffective. There appears to be insufficient appreciation of the fact that a senate or academic council is a governing body charged with oversight and acting in the best interests of the university on matters academic. By attempting to insert themselves into the governance processes and to effectively co-govern institutions, faculty associations introduce a self-interested stakeholder into the equation. In contrast, the role of labour associations is to represent their members. Faculty association members, while key university stakeholders, are not the only university stakeholders. Only occasionally will the best interests of the university align with the best interests of the one stakeholder group represented by the faculty association.

Peter MacKinnon has expressed grave concerns about whether the bicameral model is working, particularly in light of how faculty associations view their role in university governance.[23] He quotes a CAUT bulletin attributing the following statement to CAUT Executive Director, David Robinson:

> We need to protect the collegial role of our members by building provisions into our collective agreements that clearly set out where boards of governors and senates fit into the picture.[24]

MacKinnon sees this CAUT assertion as "a warning to university administrators and to provincial governments ... a reminder ... of the collective bargaining agenda that must be resisted, and of an urgent need to

---

22 Peter MacKinnon, *University Leadership and Public Policy in the Twenty-First Century* (Toronto: University of Toronto Press, 2014) at 98.
23 MacKinnon, above note 4 at 121.
24 *Ibid.*

strengthen senates as the academic voices of universities."[25] Boards must be acutely aware that their faculty associations are being pressed to involve themselves in governance. Anyone who understands key governance concepts such as fiduciary duty and conflict of interest will understand why union attempts to infiltrate governing bodies and processes represents a threat to effective university governance.

From my perspective, it's not all doom and gloom. While unionization presents challenges, faculty association activity may result in improved governance on your campus if the efforts are focused on initiatives consistent with improved governance. As a university board member, it is essential that you appreciate the tensions that arise between governance and labour relations. It is also important to retain an awareness of CAUT's views on governance, of the activity of your institution's faculty association, and of good governance practices. You are the guardian of good governance at your institution.

G. ACADEMIC FREEDOM

Boards are also charged with the protection of academic freedom, and this is another concept you will hear used and misused, debated, and discussed for years to come. It is important for board members to understand how academic freedom is defined at their institutions. In order to allow universities to fulfil their societal mission, boards must protect academic freedom. Failing to protect it, or worse yet, infringing upon it, can cause boards no end of criticism and trouble. So what is it and what purpose does it serve?

While the scope of academic freedom at your institution is likely defined in an applicable collective agreement or in an institutional policy or in both, *very* generally you should think of academic freedom as the concept that protects the academic faculty members' rights to teach and research *what they feel is important and in the way they see fit*. We all understand how important it is that judges are protected from outside influence, and in particular from political influence, so that they can be perceived to be independent, objective, and neutral. In order for academics to preserve their ability to advance and extend knowledge, they must not be vulnerable to governments or corporate entities. The integrity of their research and teaching relies on their ability to pursue the logical conclusions of the data and information they uncover and interpret, regardless of whether

---

25   *Ibid.*

those conclusions offend or irritate those in power at the university, in government, or in corporate circles. This protection is important to the advancement of knowledge generally within society. As a board member you should seek to understand academic freedom and appreciate its value so that you understand your role in protecting it.

Universities Canada's "Statement on Academic Freedom" describes what it is, why it's important, and the responsibilities it engenders. Because academic freedom is such an important concept and because the boundaries of academic freedom are tested and stretched regularly, it is worthwhile reproducing the whole Universities Canada "Statement on Academic Freedom."

What is academic freedom?

Academic freedom is the freedom to teach and conduct research in an academic environment. Academic freedom is fundamental to the mandate of universities to pursue truth, educate students and disseminate knowledge and understanding. In teaching, academic freedom is fundamental to the protection of the rights of the teacher to teach and of the student to learn. In research and scholarship, it is critical to advancing knowledge. Academic freedom includes the right to freely communicate knowledge and the results of research and scholarship.

Unlike the broader concept of freedom of speech, academic freedom must be based on institutional integrity, rigorous standards for enquiry and institutional autonomy, which allows universities to set their research and educational priorities.

Why is academic freedom important to Canada?

Academic freedom does not exist for its own sake, but rather for important social purposes. Academic freedom is essential to the role of universities in a democratic society. Universities are committed to the pursuit of truth and its communication to others, including students and the broader community. To do this, faculty must be free to take intellectual risks and tackle controversial subjects in their teaching, research and scholarship. For Canadians, it is important to know that views expressed by faculty are based on solid research, data and evidence, and that universities are autonomous and responsible institutions committed to the principles of integrity.

The responsibilities of academic freedom

Evidence and truth are the guiding principles for universities and the community of scholars that make up their faculty and students. Thus, academic freedom must be based on reasoned discourse, rigorous extensive research and scholarship, and peer review. Academic freedom is constrained by the professional standards of the relevant discipline and the responsibility of the institution to organize its academic mission. The insistence on professional standards speaks to the rigor of the enquiry and not to its outcome. The constraint of institutional requirements recognizes simply that the academic mission, like other work, has to be organized according to institutional needs. This includes the institution's responsibility to select and appoint faculty and staff, to admit and discipline students, to establish and control curriculum, to make organizational arrangements for the conduct of academic work, to certify completion of a program and to grant degrees.

Roles and responsibilities

University leadership: It is a major responsibility of university governing bodies and senior officers to protect and promote academic freedom. This includes ensuring that funding and other partnerships do not interfere with autonomy in deciding what is studied and how. Canada's university presidents must play a leadership role in communicating the values around academic freedom to internal and external stakeholders. The university must also defend academic freedom against interpretations that are excessive or too loose, and the claims that may spring from such definitions.

To ensure and protect academic freedom, universities must be autonomous, with their governing bodies committed to integrity and free to act in the institution's best interests. Universities must also ensure that the rights and freedoms of others are respected, and that academic freedom is exercised in a reasonable and responsible manner.

Faculty: Faculty must be committed to the highest ethical standards in their teaching and research. They must be free to examine data, question assumptions and be guided by evidence.

Faculty have an equal responsibility to submit their knowledge and claims to rigorous and public review by peers who are experts in the subject matter under consideration and to ground their arguments in the best available evidence.

Faculty members and university leaders have an obligation to ensure that students' human rights are respected and that they are encouraged to pursue their education according to the principles of academic freedom.

Faculty also share with university leadership the responsibility of ensuring that pressures from funding and other types of partnerships do not unduly influence the intellectual work of the university.[26]

There are many important elements to this statement, and it is worthwhile for board members to spend some time with it. I'd also recommend revisiting it from time to time as issues arise for your board.

The definition of academic freedom advanced by CAUT is much broader, and rights, rather than responsibilities, are the focus. The CAUT definition, and the approach taken to advance and expand the concept of academic freedom, is at odds with tenets of good governance. It is reproduced below.

Academic Freedom
CAUT Policy Statement

1

The institution serves the common good of society, through searching for, and disseminating, knowledge, and understanding and through fostering independent thinking and expression in academic staff and students. These ends cannot be achieved without academic freedom. All academic staff members have the right to academic freedom.

2

Academic freedom includes the right, without restriction by prescribed doctrine, to freedom to teach and discuss; freedom to carry out research and disseminate and publish the results thereof; freedom to produce and perform creative works; freedom to engage in service; freedom to express one's opinion about the institution, its administration, and the system in which one works; freedom to acquire, preserve, and provide access to documentary material in all formats; and freedom to participate in professional and representative academic bodies. Academic freedom always entails freedom from institutional censorship.

3

Academic freedom does not require neutrality on the part of the individual. Academic freedom makes intellectual discourse, critique, and

---

26 "Statement on Academic Freedom," Universities Canada (25 October 2011), online: Universities Canada www.univcan.ca/media-room/media-releases/statement-on-academic-freedom.

commitment possible. All academic staff members have the right to fulfil their functions without reprisal or suppression by the employer, the state, or any other source. Institutions have a positive obligation to defend the academic freedom rights of members.

4

All academic staff members have the right to freedom of thought, conscience, religion, expression, assembly, and association and the right to liberty and security of the person and freedom of movement. Academic staff members must not be hindered or impeded in exercising their civil rights as individuals, including the right to contribute to social change through free expression of opinion on matters of public interest. Academic staff members must not suffer any institutional penalties because of the exercise of such rights.

5

Academic staff members are entitled to have representatives on and to participate in collegial governing bodies in accordance with their role in the fulfilment of the institution's academic and educational mission. Academic staff members shall constitute at least a majority on committees or collegial governing bodies responsible for academic matters including but not limited to curriculum, assessment procedures and standards, appointment, tenure and promotion.

6

Academic freedom is a right of members of the academic staff, not of the institution. The employer shall not abridge academic freedom on any grounds, including claims of institutional autonomy.
Approved by the CAUT Council, November 2018.[27]

Boards must understand the concept of academic freedom and must understand that it is their obligation to protect academic freedom. At the same time, boards must understand that academic freedom as a concept is a political battle ground. Board members should not be intimidated by assertions that they don't understand academic freedom as these assertions may simply be efforts to impose a different or broader definition of academic freedom than is in the interests of the university and good governance.

---

27 "Academic Freedom," Canadian Association of University Teachers (November 2018), online: CAUT www.caut.ca/about-us/caut-policy/lists/caut-policy-statements/policy-statement-on-academic-freedom [endnotes omitted].

H. HOW IS ACADEMIC FREEDOM DIFFERENT FROM FREEDOM OF EXPRESSION (SPEECH)?

What is freedom of speech? Very generally, Canadians are protected against government action by a bill of rights known as the *Charter* or more completely, the *Canadian Charter of Rights and Freedoms*.[28] Under the *Charter*, all Canadians (and not just faculty members) are guaranteed certain fundamental freedoms including "freedom of thought, belief, opinion and expression, including freedom of the press and other media of communication." As noted above, the *Charter* restrains government action. This means that the actions of government, and the laws enacted by government, must respect the freedoms guaranteed by the *Charter* and can only infringe upon those rights in very specific circumstances. Generally speaking, universities are not considered government, and thus their activities are generally not governed by the *Charter*.[29] I say "generally" here because the law in this area is evolving and the applicability of the Charter to universities continues to be a live legal issue. There are cases in Alberta to the contrary, and Alberta universities are best to consult legal counsel on this point. The primary point of this discussion is to underscore the following:

- Freedom of speech is called freedom of expression in Canada. While universities should be seen to be fostering free expression for all members of their communities as a matter of public policy, universities outside of Alberta are generally not seen to be government actors, and thus not subject to the *Charter*.
- Academic freedom is different from freedom of expression or freedom of speech and includes a specific set of freedoms enjoyed by university teachers and researchers in their teaching and research.
- Board members are required first and foremost to fulfil their fiduciary duty to the university, and both their individual freedom of expression and academic freedom in the university context necessarily take a back seat to their fiduciary duty.

---

28 *Canadian Charter of Rights and Freedoms*, Part I of the *Constitution Act, 1982*, being Sched B to the *Canada Act 1982* (UK), 1982, c 11, s 2(b).

29 Atrisha S Lewis et al, "Free Speech on Campus Is Subject to the Charter — but only in Alberta" (Toronto: McCarthy Tétrault, 15 January 2020), online: www.mccarthy.ca/en/insights/blogs/canadian-appeals-monitor/free-speech-campus-subject-charter-only-alberta.

Academic members who wish to exercise academic freedom or freedom of expression in the context of their board work should not seek to serve on the university board. Their academic freedom *within* their teaching and research work continues while they serve on the board.

I. WHEN WILL BOARDS ENCOUNTER ACADEMIC FREEDOM AND FREEDOM OF EXPRESSION (SPEECH)?

In Chapter 9, during the discussion about donors as stakeholders, I noted the examples of situations in which arrangements with donors were criticized for interfering with academic freedom and university autonomy. Let's look at a couple of other examples.

Example 1

After UBC President Arvind Gupta resigned after one year in office, Jennifer Berdahl, the Montalbano Professor of Leadership Studies: Gender and Diversity at the UBC Sauder School of Business, speculated publicly about the reasons for the resignation. She expressed the views that President Gupta may have resigned because he wasn't masculine enough, or because of his lack of physical stature, and noted that he was the "first brown man" to serve as president.[30] Ms Berdahl was called by Board Chair John Montalbano (the donor whose support had created her professorship) and by another person, to discuss the blog. As a result, the UBC Faculty Association made a series of allegations against Chair Montalbano, including that he had interfered with Ms Berdahl's academic freedom. At the end of the day, this particular allegation against the board chair was not substantiated, and this case illustrates a point about academic freedom. Does academic freedom extend to anything an academic does or says? Universities Canada would say no. Peter MacKinnon also says no:

> In accusing the board chair and board of racism, sexism and lookism, Berdahl was not engaged in either teaching or research; like others she was speculating about the reasons for Gupta's departure.[31]

Instead, MacKinnon argues that Berdahl was exercising her right to free speech and the difference between academic freedom and free speech is

---

30 MacKinnon, above note 4 at 7.
31 *Ibid* at 16.

that academic freedom "bestows protection on the speaker and invokes obligations on others that are not common to [freedom of speech]."[32]

Example 2

By way of further example, consider the following. At Carleton University, Professor Root Gorelick was on the university board of governors. While on the board, he blogged about the board in derogatory terms and refused to abide by the board's code of conduct. After refusing to sign the board's code of conduct, he was found ineligible to serve a further board term. This ineligibility gave rise to multiple allegations of interference with academic freedom. These came from the Carleton University Faculty Association, CAUT, and student groups. As noted above, it is essential to good university governance that fiduciary obligation trumps academic freedom. In his chapter on this story, Peter MacKinnon states:

> [O]ne who has academic freedom as a faculty member may act in another capacity in which that same freedom is not available. Senior officers of the university are excellent examples. Most of them have academic appointments, as well as administrative offices; they retain their academic freedom for any continuing academic work they undertake, but academic freedom is not available to them with respect to their performance of administrative duties.... So too, Gorelick had academic freedom with respect to his continuing academic responsibilities but he did not have it with respect to his board membership. His obligations as a board member were to the board and its work, and his academic freedom as a faculty member cannot explain or justify his behaviour in that capacity.[33]

Although Gorelick arguably doesn't have a right of free expression as a board member to denounce the university, universities are well advised to foster and protect this freedom in members of the university community. Universities do not have an obligation, however, to protect freedom of expression or academic freedom for board members acting in their capacity as board members. Those freedoms are constrained by the board members' higher obligation — that of fiduciary duty — the obligation to act in the best interests of the university, and abide by the board code of conduct. Joining the university board is a voluntary exercise. Members of the board are subject to board rules. Members of the board are fiduciaries. Fiduciary

---

32 *Ibid* at 17.
33 *Ibid* at 73.

duty is the highest obligation of trust. Internal members who join the board and who act in a manner contrary to their fiduciary obligations will (in addition to breaching their legal obligations) be ineffective, and will contribute to a dysfunctional board. These members will foster distrust in other members, and their voices will be disregarded. In the end, internal members who work to fulfil their obligations will have influence and will be able to fulfil their intended function on the board—to bring the perspective of the faculty, staff, and students while acting in the best interests of the entire university. For more on this, I encourage you to read Peter MacKinnon's books.

I also encourage you as board members to develop an appreciation for the meaning of academic freedom. It is central to a university's role in society. Universities are places of "free inquiry" and "discovery."[34] Academics must be free to research, write about, and teach ideas that may be uncomfortable, disconcerting, unpopular, disagreeable, controversial, distasteful, impolite, and objectionable in any number of ways—they are not traditional employees. When you join a university board, you must have a sense that you are protecting and fostering this activity (researching, teaching, and learning) that advances society—an activity that sometimes pulls and sometimes yanks us forward unceremoniously to new understanding, innovation, and a deeper appreciation of the truth. Like all freedoms in civil society, however, academic freedom is not unconstrained, and understanding the limits of academic freedom are equally important to good governance.

J. CONCLUSION

Understanding the nuances of the concepts described in the chapter will make you a more effective board member. Keep in mind that the concepts are related. University autonomy is a precondition to the protection of academic freedom and university culture. An understanding of collegial culture will allow the board to engage in processes that consider all stakeholders, involve them in appropriate discussion and consultation, and create trust and foster credibility.

---

34   Austin & Jones, above note 9 at 128.

– *Part Three* –

Good Governance in Action

CHAPTER 12

Understanding Your University's Governance Structure

As every university in Canada is different, this chapter will provide an overview of the legislation that creates universities, the role of the bylaws, and policy. University legislation almost always establishes the board's composition. The unique composition of each university board is an aspect of university governance that creates the basis for a dynamic and successful board culture.

A. GOVERNING FRAMEWORK: LEGISLATION AND BYLAWS

It's helpful to think of your university's legislative and governance framework as a hierarchy. The source of all authority is the document that created the university. As described above, while many universities have their own acts and charters, some provinces (Alberta and British Columbia) have one piece of legislation that applies to multiple universities.[1] There is a small list of universities that were created by royal or papal charter prior to 1867.[2] Many of these have subsequently been continued by a piece of provincial

---

1   *Post-Secondary Learning Act*, SA 2003, c P-19.5; *University Act*, RSBC 1996, c 468.
2   Theresa Shanahan, Michelle Nilson & Li-Jeen Broshko, *Handbook of Canadian Higher Education Law* (Kingston: School of Policy Studies, Queen's University, 2015) at 41. This list includes: University of King's College, Nova Scotia; McGill University, Quebec; King's College (University of Toronto), Ontario; University of Laval, Quebec; Queen's

legislation. With the exception of the Royal Military College (RMC) and Queen's University at Kingston, all other universities were created by individual acts of provincial legislation. RMC is the only university created by an act of the federal parliament. Queen's University at Kingston continues to be governed by its Royal Charter, and amendments to the charter must be approved by the federal parliament, rather than by the provincial parliament.[3] For the rest of this chapter, I'll refer to the document that creates your university, whether it be an act or a charter, as your "legislation."

As noted above, your legislation is the source of all authority within the university. If the legislation is the top level, the university bylaws are at the next lower level, followed by other documents such as committee terms of reference and policies. The authority is dispersed as it falls. Lower levels of authority always have to be consistent with higher levels. Policies must be consistent with bylaws and bylaws must be consistent with the legislation. To the extent that any of these documents is inconsistent with a higher-level document, it is invalid.

Think about the bylaws as filling in the details not addressed in the legislation, and think about policies and procedures as furnishing more details. While you can rely on your board professional to be familiar with the legislation or charter, take time to familiarize yourself with what is in the charter or act. Go back and review it once in a while; as you learn more about the institution, these documents will have more meaning. I have the same advice with respect to the university bylaws.

One could be forgiven for thinking that university legislation is all the same. But it is not. While there are a lot of structural similarities, each university is distinct. Universities are created by different pieces of legislation, and the legislation does differ significantly from university to university. Even those universities in British Columbia[4] and Alberta that are created

---

University at Kingston, Ontario; Trinity College (University of Toronto), Ontario; Bishop's University, Quebec; and University of Ottawa, Ontario.

3   Queen's University, *Consolidated Royal Charter*, 2001, online: www.queensu.ca/secretariat/royal-charter.

4   The British Columbia *University Act*, above note 1, governs University of British Columbia, University of Victoria, Simon Fraser University, and University of Northern British Columbia. Other universities in the province have their own legislation. For example, Thompson Rivers University has its own act and on its homepage notes that it is also governed by the *University Act*: "TRU was established by an act of the British Columbia Provincial Legislature, the Thompson Rivers University Act, in 2005. Leadership and degree-granting powers of the university are also legislated by British Columbia's University Act," online: www.tru.ca/about/accreditation.html.

by common legislation superimpose that on institutions with different traditions and practices. For this reason, as much as I'd like to be able to explain your legislation and bylaws to you, that's another book. (Although it's probably a book few would read!) I can, however, give you a sense of what is generally in university legislation:

1) An overview of your institution's purpose, mission, and high-level objectives
2) A description of the governance framework
   i. Creation of the governing board (board of trustees, board of regents, or board of governors) and a description of its composition
   ii. Role and powers of the board
   iii. Information about board member obligations, roles of board leaders, terms, conflict of interest, etc.
   iv. Relationship between the board and the academic governing body
   v. Creation of the academic governing body (senate, academic council, university council, general faculties council)
   vi. Role and powers of the academic governing body
3) Provision for the offices of university officers such as the president and chancellor
4) Rules about meetings
5) The power to enact bylaws
6) Financial matters, including the requirement for annual audits, tax exempt status, borrowing powers, the power to own land, protection from governmental powers of expropriation, and granting the university powers of expropriation

There may be many more provisions in your legislation. Some legislation is much more detailed than others, and many pieces of legislation leave the detail to the bylaws.

B. UNIVERSITY POLICIES

Boards should also be guided by university policy. Because universities are complex places, the policy framework is unlikely to be simple, particularly if the university is older. A good policy framework categorizes university policies and clarifies consultation and approval paths. Boards will have their own policies and procedures relating to the conduct of the board and board members. Familiarizing yourself with them is important. They will address conduct and attendance, eligibility, and other board practices. But there are also important institutional policies with which the board should be familiar, including signing authority and approval, contract management, risk management, code of ethics, policies against harassment, discrimination and sexual violence, information governance, privacy, and more. Here again, your governance professional will have a key role to play in ensuring that the board understands how to navigate the policy framework, and what the key policies are. The board or board committee should be advised of any policies that have a bearing on any board or committee decision. An annual report on policies is also a good idea, because it's also the board's role to ensure that significant policy gaps are filled.

C. BOARD COMPOSITION

A unique aspect of university governance is the composition of the university governing board. As noted above, your university legislation establishes the board composition. In addition to community or independent members, university boards generally have members from key stakeholder groups, including faculty, staff, and students, among others. These members are considered internal members. The composition of your board will be one of the other things that sets your university apart, as your composition will reflect the importance of key stakeholders. For example, in addition to key internal stakeholders, you may see other key internal/external stakeholders such as members of Indigenous communities, local municipal figures, or individuals from another institution. Table 12.1 provides an overview of the composition of a sample of eight different universities. These universities were selected to demonstrate the diverse composition of Canadian university boards.

Table 12.1 Board Composition of Sample Universities

Source of Members	University of Calgary	St. Francis Xavier University	Memorial University of Newfoundland	McGill University	Algoma University	Lakehead University	University of Waterloo	University of Ontario Institute of Technology
Total Maximum Voting Members	25	45	30	25	30	30	36	25
President and Vice-Chancellor/Rector	1	1	1	1	1	1	1	1
Chancellor	1	1	1	1	1		1	1
Faculty	2	4		2	1			2
Academic Governing Body	2			2		1	7	
Student (Undergraduate and Graduate)	2	3	4	2	2	1	5	1
Persons Appointed by the Bishop		2						
Non-academic Staff	2			2	1	1	2	1
Lieutenant Governor In Council Appointees			17		3	3	7	3
Bishop		1						
Alumni	3	2	6	3	1	1	3	

Dark grey denotes student members. Light grey denotes internal members.

Source of Members	University of Calgary	St. Francis Xavier University	Memorial University of Newfoundland	McGill University	Algoma University	Lakehead University	University of Waterloo	University of Ontario Institute of Technology
Municipal Government						1	3	
Partner Institution								6
Indigenous Community or Government					4	1		
University Secretary		1						
Persons Elected by Priests		6						
External/Community/Members at Large	12	21		12	8[5]	20	7	10
Provost or Other Vice-President		2	1					
Appointee of Affiliated Institution		1						

Dark grey denotes student members. Light grey denotes internal members.

5 The university website shows 8 external representatives currently. Two of these members would also fall into the LGIC category above. The university may — but is not required to — appoint all 30 voting members.

D. EFFECTIVE MANAGEMENT OF A BOARD THAT INCLUDES INTERNAL MEMBERS

Board members who come from the corporate sector in Canada find it unusual that university boards have internal members on them. While worker representation on corporate boards is seen in Germany, having employees (other than the Chief Executive Officer) on an organization's board is not common in North America. As can be seen from Table 12.1, all of the sample universities have at least one employee in addition to the president and vice-chancellor sitting on the board. Most of them have both faculty and staff on the board. All of the universities have student board members. In North America, where the corporate governance focus is on independent oversight and avoidance of conflict of interest, board members sometimes struggle with having internal university members sitting on the board. This struggle happens for a number of reasons:

1) Internal board members may perceive themselves as "representing" the constituency from which they came. This perception is accentuated by selection processes that see internal board members running against others and being selected by a vote of the constituency or body from which they came.
2) Internal board members may focus on the interests of the constituency from which they came and not on the best interests of the university.
3) External board members may perceive internal board members as having an "agenda" and unable to act in the interests of the university as a whole.

When any of these things happen, internal board members will be marginalized and board culture and engagement will be damaged. In Chapter 11, we looked at former Carleton University faculty board member Root Gorelick in the context of the limits of academic freedom. The same example serves to illustrate the damage that can be done to board culture by an internal member who puts other interests first. As Peter MacKinnon states:

> It is not possible to capture here the full impact of these attacks by Gorelick on his board colleagues. Reading them in the context of the entire blog leads to the conclusion that the board was deflected from its normal agendas to deal with the attacks and their fallout, including the protracted procedural debates to which they led. This deflection did not last for a week or two, but for more than a year. That is a serious problem in itself, given the importance to the university, and to the public, of the

effective and efficient discharge of board duties.... Attacks of this kind are felt by other board members and have a deleterious effect on board meetings. Trust and civility are important to boards, and they can be undermined by the conduct of only one of their members.[6]

MacKinnon posits that Gorelick's behaviour could only have been based on a "misunderstanding of his role":

His reference to his constituents; his orientation to due process rather than to the due diligence that is required of boards; and his comparison of the board to a parliament with elected members; and presumably an official opposition of which he was the leader or a member, all suggest that he did not understand board governance.[7]

While I acknowledge that there is no easy answer to what Peter MacKinnon describes as the "constituency factor,"[8] there are things that can be done to address the perceived conflict of interest.

- Ensure that internal board members are best positioned to bring the perspective of the constituent group but avoid acting as a representative.
- Make it clear to internal members what the role of a board member is even before they make a decision to seek a position on the board.
- Manage the selection process so that even if representatives are selected through voting, there is no campaigning. The selection is based on credentials and interest in the governance process.
- Use every opportunity to educate all members about their fiduciary duties, avoidance of conflict of interest, and the obligation to act in the best interests of the university. Training and orientation sessions are only a start. The board chair should set the tone at every meeting.
- Manage the performance of board members. The board chair should develop a relationship with internal members and take opportunities to guide the members to act in the best interests of the

---

6   Peter MacKinnon, *University Commons Divided: Exploring Debate & Dissent on Campus* (Toronto: University of Toronto Press, 2018) at 65.
7   *Ibid* at 64.
8   *Ibid* at 62.

university. Enforce a culture of respectful dialogue and debate at the board table.
- The board chair and the governance professional should plan meetings and social events, ensuring the equal treatment of all board members, making certain there are no hallway discussions and gatherings of only external members, and avoiding giving recognition or opportunities only to external members.

1) Other Stakeholder Appointees

As Table 12.1 illustrates, university boards may also include appointees from other stakeholder communities. Some of the same issues arise here as they do for the internal appointees. Do members from stakeholder communities understand that they come to bring the perspective of a particular constituency but not to represent a constituency? A further challenge with stakeholder appointees is that their selection is usually out of the governing board's control. While the external members chosen by the board are selected based on a skills matrix with a view to recruiting a diverse group of members with specific sector backgrounds and specific types of experience, other stakeholder members are appointed, and they may or may not understand good governance or fulfil requirements on the skills matrix. Having stakeholder appointees may also limit the board's ability to fully implement good diversity, equity, and inclusion practices.

It is essential to an effective board that all board members have an equal voice at the board table. Significant board dysfunction can ensue if the board allows divisions among internal, stakeholder, and external board members.

As noted above, there are several practical ways to address these issues, but the bottom line is that board members who bring the valuable perspective of the internal constituency and who demonstrate a clear understanding of the role of the board and their fiduciary obligations to act in the best interests of the university will be respected by fellow board members and will have a voice. Those who cannot separate or rise above their individual interests and confuse their interests with the best interests of the university, or who use their board seats as a podium for advancing specific personal or single-stakeholder interests will be marginalized, ignored, and ineffective. They will also cause a rift on the board that will lead to board dysfunction and the disengagement of board members who are there to act in the best interests of the university.

E. COMPOSITION OF ACADEMIC GOVERNING BODIES

Reproduced below is a table prepared by Lea Pennock et al listing the voting members of academic governing bodies of bicameral Canadian universities. As they note, the sizes of senates vary widely; an average size is about seventy-seven members, the largest having 200 members and the smallest fewer than twenty-five members.[9] On average, faculty members make up 48 percent of total academic governing body membership; the next two largest groups represented are students (16 percent) and deans (13 percent).[10] Most senates number the president, vice-presidents, and provost, as well as deans, among voting members. Eighty-four percent of academic governing bodies are chaired by the university president.[11] Table 12.2 provides additional membership information.

Table 12.2 Voting Members of Academic Governing Bodies of Bicameral Canadian Universities[12]

Membership Category	Percentage of All Senate Members	Percentage of Senates Reporting Members in This Category
Faculty	48.0	100.0
Students	16.0	98.0
Deans (ex officio)	13.0	93.0
Other senior administrators	5.0	80.0
Department heads (ex officio)	5.0	24.0
Vice-presidents or provost	4.0	95.0
Members of affiliated or federated institutions	2.0	42.0
Alumni	2.0	42.0
President	1.0	97.0
Non-academic staff	1.0	39.0
Members of the board of governors (ex officio)	1.0	39.0

---

9   Lea Pennock et al, "Academic Senates and University Governance in Canada: Changes in Structure and Perceptions of Senate Members" (Paper presented at the annual meeting of the Consortium of Higher Education Researchers, Belgrade, Serbia, 10–12 September 2012) at 5.
10 Ibid.
11 Ibid at 6.
12 Ibid.

Membership Category	Percentage of All Senate Members	Percentage of Senates Reporting Members in This Category
Chancellor	0.7	55.0
Bargaining-unit representatives	0.4	16.0
Government representatives	0.2	13.0
Other	2.0	42.0

The size and composition of academic governing bodies are challenges to effective bicameral governance and effective relationships between the academic governing body and the board of governors at any given institution. The size of many academic governing bodies creates communication challenges and education challenges. It also inhibits the working relationship between the board and the academic governing body. Only 1 percent of senate members are drawn from their university boards, and only 39 percent of academic governing bodies have a board member on them. Add to this fact that the board and academic governing bodies may have two separate governance offices, and you have two entirely separate silos.

F. PROMOTING EFFECTIVE WORKING RELATIONSHIPS WITH ACADEMIC GOVERNING BODIES

Effective governance requires eradicating silos and bridging the divide between the board and the academic governing body that exists in most institutions. There is no easy fix, but two things will help: (1) improving awareness of the academic governing body's role as a governing body of the institution (such as a duty to act in the best interests of the university as a whole), and (2) developing a common objective to improve governance within both governing bodies. As far as I know, this isn't happening right now, but the work of Lea Pennock et al (cited above) on the effectiveness of senates provides some cause for hope, as it reveals that senate members themselves are aware of the gap between what they think they should be doing and what they are doing. Academic governing bodies should be building on this work to improve their governance practices. Universities can continue to build from there. In Chapter 14, there will be more discussion about academic governing body effectiveness.

CHAPTER 13

The Roles of the Board and the Academic Governing Body

In the previous chapter, you were given an overview of university legislation, its components, and the challenges that university board composition presents. In this chapter, we will step back a little to view the roles of the university board and the academic governing body generally before returning to examine the powers given to both within university legislation. We will review the relationship between the board and the academic governing body, and conclude by looking at the challenges to bicameral governance arising from the effectiveness of the academic governing body.

A. THE ROLE OF THE UNIVERSITY BOARD: THE BIGGER PICTURE

I have learned a lot since I began writing this book, one of the most important things being the significant role that the university board plays in preserving institutional autonomy and the institution's right to self-governance. As much as those working for universities (scholars and administrators) may scoff and chafe at being overseen by a body whose membership includes individuals from outside of the sector, universities are public bodies, supported by public funds, and they must act in the public interest. As Peter MacKinnon says, "[s]elf-governance is possible in public institutions only if its mechanisms and behaviours are compatible with sound governance principles that adequately protect the public interest."[1] Both the board and the academic governing body must be mindful of the important connection between institutional autonomy and good governance. It is only if the governing bodies of the university demonstrate effectiveness in protecting the public interest that governments will entrust continued oversight to them. While it is true that this responsibility primarily falls to the board, the board cannot govern effectively without a fully functioning academic governing body also committed to good governance.

As all those employed within an institution are fundamentally in a conflict of interest, good governance demands external oversight. If an independent board of governors does not have supervision, then who? The likely answer is the government. As discussed in Chapter 8 and again in Chapter 16, governments are becoming increasingly involved in universities by making policy decisions that effectively usurp the role of the board. Tuition controls and the imposition of performance-management metrics are but two examples. There are many more.

So how do boards preserve institutional autonomy and the continued right of institutional self-governance? In the first instance, boards (and all key stakeholders) have to appreciate that preserving institutional autonomy is the first order of business. Effective governance demonstrates that an institution is soundly and responsibly run, and is the most important means to preserving institutional autonomy. Achieving and maintaining highly effective governance has to be a top board priority.

Best Practice Tips: Some Suggestions for Maintaining Highly Effective University Governance

- Employ an experienced governance professional reporting to the president and the board chair.
- Conduct annual board practices assessments in which specific questions are asked about all aspects of governance.
- Benchmark: Look both outside and inside the sector for governance best practices. Although those inside the sector are highly suspicious of corporate governance best practices, universities are not models of good governance generally, and many corporate governance best practices are principles-based, and as such transcend sector.

---

1 Peter MacKinnon, *University Leadership and Public Policy in the Twenty-First Century: A President's Perspective* (Toronto: University of Toronto Press, 2014) at 92.

- Use benchmarking information and the results of the board practices assessments to develop long- and short-term governance plans. Actively work on these plans — measure and report on them.
- Take steps to promote an effective working relationship with the academic governing body and encourage that body to understand the importance of its role as a governing body within the institution, and to adopt good governance practices itself.
- Engage your board members and create a culture in which high performance is expected. Use self-assessment tools to continually improve the culture. Offer board members peer mentoring, educational opportunities, and reinforce their fiduciary obligations. Ensure that board members have opportunities to learn about your institution.
- While governing in the interests of the institution, ensure that your board understands and considers its stakeholders and their interests each time significant decisions are made.

B. KEY FUNCTIONS OF THE UNIVERSITY BOARD

University legislation will include a list of board responsibilities. You should familiarize yourself with that list. It's also important to understand the broad categories of responsibilities of university boards. Primary functions of a university board include:

- establishing and maintaining a relevant mission and keeping the mission alive by ensuring that strategy and planning align with the mission
- ensuring that the mission reflects and protects the public interest
- hiring and managing the president
- overseeing the establishment of a sound strategic plan and monitoring and measuring it
- ensuring that there is a university risk-management program and keeping the board apprised of risk-management activities at least annually
- ensuring that there is a compliance program and keeping the board apprised of compliance-management activities at least annually
- taking steps to understand and promote a positive university culture — from employee morale to ensuring an equitable, diverse, and inclusive environment
- ensuring financial sustainability

- supporting and engaging in university advancement activities (fundraising and university promotion)
- overseeing mechanisms for ensuring educational quality
- protecting academic freedom
- ensuring the existence of a clear authority structure, including a policy framework
- engaging with and understanding the interests of all university stakeholders, and demonstrating this engagement in decision-making, and through interaction and communication
- setting the tone at the top with respect to the university values, ethics, and integrity[2]

C. BOARD POWERS

Your university legislation sets out the powers of the board and is the source of all the powers needed to oversee the university. Appendix 13.1 sets out sample clauses from the legislation of five universities from across the country: University of Waterloo (ON), Mount Allison University (NB), Bishop's University (QC), University of Winnipeg (MB), as well as the overarching legislation applying to universities in British Columbia. I categorized the general powers given to boards and the results were fascinating.

Appendix 13.1 illustrates that university legislation commonly delegates the following types of powers to governing boards:

1) general powers to oversee the university and make all of the decisions necessary to do so
2) powers of appointment, compensation, and management of the president and of any or all of the academic and non-academic staff; powers over terms and conditions of employment; power to grant tenure to faculty
3) power to borrow money and pledge security
4) power to set tuition and fees for students, and power to regulate student conduct, as well as the conduct of other university members

---

2   Although these are the author's words, the original source of key parts of this list is the Association of Governing Boards of Colleges and Universities (AGB). The AGB is a member-based organization operating in the United States. Although US-focused, it is the source of vast amounts of information about US university governance and issues facing universities there. While US and Canadian universities operate in different contexts, there are many common themes and dynamics

5) power to enter into agreements
6) power to affiliate with other institutions
7) power to invest
8) power to make rules about various matters, including rules and procedures relating to the conduct of its own proceedings
9) power to acquire and govern university property
10) power to enact bylaws
11) power to determine and delegate authority
12) power to grant degrees
13) power to set or approve academic organizational structure
14) power to approve the strategic plan
15) obligation to oversee finances and power to approve the budget.

Note that where the legislation for your university may be less specific, or may not include some of the above powers, the source of the board's authority may be found in the delegation of general power to oversee the university. Further, some of the powers may be specified in the university's bylaws (essentially, regulations approved by the board that implement and specify the university's legislation). It is good practice for the board and board committees to cite the legislative source of their authority when making a decision.

Best Practice Tip: An easy way to ensure consistent and clear linkages to board or committee authority is to have the university adopt a standard board and board-committee memo that includes a section setting out the source of the board or committee's authority or responsibility with respect to the item being presented.

Your board orientation session will likely include an overview of the university legislation and bylaws, but familiarity comes with regular review. Although I am very familiar with my university's legislation, I go back to my university's act and bylaws regularly each time I encounter a new issue; it's a good idea for you to do the same.

D. THE NAME OF THE ACADEMIC GOVERNING BODY

Your university legislation also creates, names, empowers, and establishes obligations for your university's academic governing body. As noted above, unless you have a unicameral institution, these academic governing bodies at different institutions have different names, too. "Senate" is the most common name, but you will also hear the academic governing body called "academic council," "university council," and "general faculties council."

E. THE PURVIEW OF THE ACADEMIC GOVERNING BODY

Simply put, the purview of the academic governing body is academic matters. In some cases, "purview" means exclusive jurisdiction and in others "purview" is subject to varying degrees of board oversight. University legislation and bylaws will govern the degree of board oversight over the work of the academic governing body and also govern the scope of what is considered the "academic realm" within a given institution.

In the next section of this chapter, we'll be reviewing the delegation of power to the academic governing body, and this will give you more of a sense of the types of decisions that fall within the academic realm. Generally speaking, however, academic matters are "matters relating to teaching and learning."[3] In addition to this primary role, "[m]ost university senates play at least some role in decisions related to research policy, strategic planning, and the budget process."[4] With respect to research policy, some senates have final approval authority, while others will review the policy before sending it to the board for final approval. Senates have varying roles in strategic planning: approximately 30 percent approve and then send to the board for approval; 25 percent play an advisory role to the board; a small percentage endorses the plan before it proceeds to the board; a small percentage appoints members to a strategic-planning body. The majority of senates (66 percent) play an advisory role in the budget process,[5] others receive the budget for information. There is one example of a senate with power to approve the budget, but even in that case, the board retains the ultimate authority to approve the budget as the failure to secure that approval results in the board having to approve the budget by a two-thirds majority vote.[6]

---

3   Lea Pennock et al, "Academic Senates and University Governance in Canada: Changes in Structure and Perceptions of Senate Members" (Paper presented at the annual meeting of the Consortium of Higher Education Researchers, Belgrade, Serbia, 10–12 September 2012) at 9.
4   *Ibid* at 9.
5   *Ibid* at 10.
6   *Ibid*.

F. POWERS OF THE ACADEMIC GOVERNING BODY

Appendix 13.2 lists the categories of university-legislated powers and obligations of the academic governing bodies at the same five randomly chosen universities listed in Section C. Some common delegations of authority to academic governing bodies include the following general areas:

1) responsibility to give recommendations or advice on a wide variety of matters to the governing board or others
2) general academic governance
3) academic programming and courses of study
4) degree-granting powers
5) powers with respect to academic organization
6) faculty appointments and promotions (either authority to appoint or to approve the policies governing appointment)
7) awards, scholarships and bursaries
8) admissions policies and standards
9) examinations policies and standards
10) discipline for student academic or other misconduct, and appeals from the same
11) powers to establish policies, bylaws, and rules for the conduct of its own affairs/governance
12) financial, resource, or other budgetary advisory responsibility
13) powers respecting affiliation of the university with other institutions and the governance of the same

Remember that the academic governing body's role is to make decisions on academic matters. Of course, the lines between administrative, executive, and academic matters can be indistinct, and again, each university's legislation defines the roles differently.

G. CONCLUSION

This chapter is intended to provide context for better understanding the specific relationship between or among the governing bodies at your institution. Understanding how university governance works generally will assist you in understanding your university governance model. These are the first steps toward building or maintaining effective governance at your university.

APPENDIX 13.1
A Sample of Powers Delegated to Governing Boards in Five Pieces of Legislation

Category of Delegated Power	University of Waterloo Act (all references to section 14(1))[1]	Mount Allison University Act[2]	Statutes of Bishop's University[3]	University of Winnipeg Act[4]	University Act (applies to BC universities)[5]
Name of governing body	Board of Governors	Board of Regents	Board of Governors	Board of Regents	Board of Governors
General powers	14.(1) The government of the University and the control of its property and revenues, the conduct of its business and affairs, save with respect to such matters as are assigned by this Act to the Senate, shall be vested in the Board of Governors	4. (i) subject to the express provisions of this Act, to exercise all or any of the incidental and ancillary powers conferred upon companies by the Companies Act of the Province of New Brunswick as from time to time in force;	Division 1, Section 1, 1.1: The overall management of the affairs of the University is vested in a Board of Governors. The Board of Governors shall be responsible for general oversight and policymaking.	12 (1) The board has overall responsibility for the university, and may determine all matters of university policy except those specifically assigned to the senate by this Act.	27 (1) The management, administration and control of the property, revenue, business and affairs of the university are vested in the board.

1 https://uwaterloo.ca/secretariat/governance/university-waterloo-act#Powers-of-Board-of-Governors.
2 www.mta.ca/Community/Governance_and_admin/Governance/Board_of_Regents/Mount_Allison_University_Act/Mount_Allison_University_Act.
3 www.ubishops.ca/wp-content/uploads/200501_Statutes-Bishops-University-approved-by-the-Board-of-Governors.pdf.
4 www.uwinnipeg.ca/regents/uofw-act.pdf.
5 www.bclaws.gov.bc.ca/civix/document/id/complete/statreg/96468_01#section2.

Category of Delegated Power	University of Waterloo Act (section 14(1))	Mount Allison University Act	Statutes of Bishop's University	University of Winnipeg Act	University Act (applies to BC universities)
General powers	and the Board of Governors shall have all powers necessary or convenient to perform its duties and to achieve the objects of the University …	4. (j) to do all things reasonably incidental to the carrying out of the foregoing powers, rights, privileges and objects. 8 (1) The management and control of the business and affairs of the University shall be vested in a Board of Regents.	Division II, Section 1: The functions and powers of the Board of Governors include the following: 1.1.1 ensuring that the University's mission, values and principles are respected, having a superintending and reforming power over all decisions affecting activities held at the University or connected with the University.	12 (2) (o) do any other thing that the board considers necessary or advisable to carry out the objects and purposes of the university under this Act.	

Appendix 13.1

Category of Delegated Power	University of Waterloo Act (section 14(1))	Mount Allison University Act	Statutes of Bishop's University	University of Winnipeg Act	University Act (applies to BC universities)
Powers of appointment — president, academic or non-academic staff, power to grant tenure to faculty, terms and conditions of employment, performance management	(a) to appoint, promote and remove the President and all other officers of the University, heads and associate heads of the faculties, or of any other academic unit, the members of faculty, or staff of the University, and all other agents and servants of the University; (b) to grant tenure to members of faculty, and to terminate tenure.		Division 2, Section 1: 1.6 ensuring the applicant recruiting process to fill the position of Principal and Vice-Chancellor of the University provides an equal opportunity for applicants from outside and from within the University and that the procedure allows for the external and confidential examination of applications. Division 2, Section 1: 1.8 approving the criteria for evaluating the performance of the Principal and	12 (2) (a) appoint the president of the university and determine his or her term of office and remuneration; (b) engage academic and other staff as required, determine their duties and conditions of employment, and set their salaries and honoraria.	27 (2) (f) with the approval of the senate, to establish procedures for the recommendation and selection of candidates for president, deans, librarians, registrar and other senior academic administrators as the board may designate; (g) subject to section 28, to appoint the president of the university, deans of all faculties, the librarian, the registrar, the bursar, the professors, associate professors, assistant professors,

Category of Delegated Power	University of Waterloo Act (section 14(1))	Mount Allison University Act	Statutes of Bishop's University	University of Winnipeg Act	University Act (applies to BC universities)
Powers of appointment			Vice-Chancellor of the University.		lecturers, instructors and other members of the teaching staff of the university, and the officers and employees the board considers necessary for the purpose of the university, and to set their salaries or remuneration, and to define their duties and their tenure of office or employment.
			Division 2, Section 1: 1.9 coming to an agreement with the Principal and Vice-Chancellor on the objectives to be achieved and determining the Principal and Vice-Chancellor's compensation.	12 (2) (n) establish pension and other plans, either contributory or non-contributory, to provide retirement and other benefits for employees of the university.	27 (2) (h) if the president is absent or unable to act, or if there is a vacancy in that office, to appoint an acting president.

Appendix 13.1 131

Category of Delegated Power	University of Waterloo Act (section 14(1))	Mount Allison University Act	Statutes of Bishop's University	University of Winnipeg Act	University Act (applies to BC universities)
Power to borrow money and pledge security	(d) to borrow money for the purpose of the University and to give security therefor on such terms and in such amounts as the said Board of Governors may consider advisable, or as from time to time may be required.	6 The University, if authorized by by-law or resolution of the Board, may (a) borrow money on its credit in such amount, on such terms and from such persons, firms or corporations, including chartered banks, as may be determined or approved by the Board; (b) make, draw and endorse promissory notes or bills of exchange; (c) mortgage, hypothecate, pledge or charge any part or all of the property of the University to secure	Board of Governors must approve. See 12.2.6 below in "Power to enter into agreements."	12 (2) (f) borrow money that may, in any fiscal year, be required to meet the ordinary expenditures of the university until the revenues for that year are available, and, with the approval of the Lieutenant Governor in Council, borrow money for any other purpose.	31 (1) The board may, by resolution, borrow money required to meet the expenditures of the university until the revenues of the current year are available. (2) Money borrowed under subsection (1) must be repaid out of current revenues and may be secured by promissory notes of the university. 58 (1) With the approval of the minister and Minister of Finance, a university may borrow money for the purpose of

Category of Delegated Power	University of Waterloo Act (section 14(1))	Mount Allison University Act	Statutes of Bishop's University	University of Winnipeg Act	University Act (applies to BC universities)
Power to borrow money and pledge security		any money borrowed or the fulfillment of the obligations incurred by the University under any promissory note or bill of exchange signed, made, drawn or endorsed by it; (d) issue bonds, debentures and obligations on such terms and conditions as the Board may decide or approve, and pledge or sell such bonds, debentures and obligations for such sums and at such prices as the Board may decide or approve, and mortgage, hypothecate, pledge or charge all or any part of the property of the University to secure any such bonds, debentures and obligations.			(a) purchasing or otherwise acquiring land for the use of the university, or (b) erecting, repairing, adding to, furnishing or equipping any building or other structure for the use of the university. (2) The board may (a) enter into any agreement that it may consider necessary or advisable for carrying out the purposes mentioned in this section, and (b) execute in the name of the university all agreements, deeds and other instruments considered necessary or advisable to carry into effect the provisions of the agreement.

Appendix 13.1

Category of Delegated Power	University of Waterloo Act (section 14(1))	Mount Allison University Act	Statutes of Bishop's University	University of Winnipeg Act	University Act (applies to BC universities)
Power to set tuition and fees for students and the power to regulate student conduct	(e) to regulate the conduct of the students, faculty and staff, and of all other persons coming upon and using the lands and premises of the University. (f) to establish and collect fees and charges for academic tuition and for services of any kind which may be offered by the University and to collect such fees and charges, approved by the Board of Governors, on behalf of any entity, organization, or element of the University.			12 (2) (I) set fees and all other charges to be paid to the university. 12 (2) (d) exercise internal disciplinary jurisdiction over the non-academic conduct of students, including the power to expel or suspend for cause.	27 (m) to set, determine and collect the fees (i) to be paid for instruction, research and all other activities in the university, (ii) for extramural instruction, (iii) for public lecturing, library fees, and laboratory fees, (iv) for examinations, degrees and certificates, (v) for the use of any student or alumni organization in charge of student or alumni activities, and (vi) for the building and operation of a gymnasium or other athletic facilities.

Category of Delegated Power	University of Waterloo Act (section 14(1))	Mount Allison University Act	Statutes of Bishop's University	University of Winnipeg Act	University Act (applies to BC universities)
Power to set tuition and fees for students and the power to regulate student conduct	(g) to levy and enforce penalties and fines, suspend or expel from student membership or from employment with the University or deny access to the lands and premises of the University.				
Power to enter into agreements	Not specified.	Not specified.	Division 2, Section 12: 12.1 General Authority — The Board of Governors has the general and overriding power to enter into all contracts binding the University. It retains such power, notwithstanding the delegation of authority conferred upon specified delegates in any signing authority resolution passed by it from time to time.	12 (2) (h) enter into agreements or arrangements to further the university's purposes and objects, and designating the appropriate signing officers for agreements and other documents.	27 (s) to enter into agreements on behalf of the university.

Appendix 13.1

Category of Delegated Power	University of Waterloo Act (section 14(1))	Mount Allison University Act	Statutes of Bishop's University	University of Winnipeg Act	University Act (applies to BC universities)
Power to enter into agreements	Not specified.	Not specified.	Division 2, Section 12: 12.2 External Matters Requiring Board Approval Without limiting the generality of Section 12.1, the following external matters require the approval of the Board of Governors: 12.2.1 any contract, agreement or obligation that, in the opinion of the Principal and Vice-Chancellor or responsible Officer, should be approved by the Board of Governors, regardless of value; 12.2.2 any real estate transaction.	12 (2) (l) enter into any arrangement with a governmental authority in Canada with respect to giving assistance to a college or university outside Canada by supplying teaching staff, supervising staff, or otherwise. 12 (2) (k) enter into agreements with any incorporated society or association in the province that has power to prescribe examinations for admission to, or registration with, the society or association, concerning conducting examinations, prescribing courses of study and providing instruction.	

Category of Delegated Power	University of Waterloo Act (section 14(I))	Mount Allison University Act	Statutes of Bishop's University	University of Winnipeg Act	University Act (applies to BC universities)
Power to enter into agreements			12.2.3 any lease contract or agreement for a term that exceeds five (5) years; 12.2.4 any contract or agreement obligating the University and involving an aggregate amount exceeding $500,000; 12.2.5 any contract or agreement that the Board of Governors, by resolution, requests be brought to the Board of Governors for approval; 12.2.6 any contract or agreement to borrow money;	12 (2) (j) enter into agreements with any incorporated society or association in the province to establish and maintain a joint system of instruction.	

Appendix 13.1

Category of Delegated Power	University of Waterloo Act (section 14(1))	Mount Allison University Act	Statutes of Bishop's University	University of Winnipeg Act	University Act (applies to BC universities)
Power to enter into agreements			12.2.7 any research or special project contract or agreement resulting in additional costs to the university of $100,000 or more.		
Power to affiliate with other institutions	(i) to enter into agreements for the federation or affiliation of the University with any university or college of higher learning.	4 (d) to procure or promote the affiliation with the University of any other college or other educational institution.	Division 1, Section 5: 5.15 Colleges and Schools which fulfil adequate conditions of teaching and control may be affiliated to the University by action of the Board of Governors under such terms and conditions as the Senate may prescribe.	12 (2) (m) either on the recommendation of the senate or on the board's own initiative after consultation with the senate, authorize affiliation between the university and other academic institutions.	
Power to invest	Not specified.	(h) to invest and reinvest any funds of the University not otherwise required for its immediate purposes, subject to any trust or		12 (2) (g) subject to the limitations imposed by any trust, invest money belonging to the university, or held by it in trust, in	57 Subject to a contrary intent expressed in a gift, devise, bequest or trust, section 15 of the *Trustee Act* does not apply to

Category of Delegated Power	University of Waterloo Act (section 14(1))	Mount Allison University Act	Statutes of Bishop's University	University of Winnipeg Act	University Act (applies to BC universities)
Power to invest		condition affecting the same.		any kind of property, whether real, personal or mixed, exercising the judgment and care that a person of prudence, discretion and intelligence would exercise in administering the property of others.	investments made by a board of a university and each board (a) may invest money belonging to the university and available for investment, and (b) must, when investing under paragraph (a), make investments that a prudent person would make.
Power to make rules about various matters, including rules and procedures relating to the conduct of its own proceedings	Not specified.	Not specified.	Division 1, Section 11.4: The Board of Governors ... and any of their respective committees may establish their own internal policies and procedures which shall be supplementary, but not contradictory, to those contained in these Statutes.	12 (2) (e) establish rules and procedures for the conduct of its own proceedings, including establishing standing and other committees and determining when and in what manner meetings of the board and standing committees	27 (2) Without limiting subsection (1) or the general powers conferred on the board by this Act, the board has the following powers: (a) to make rules for the meetings of the board and its transactions;

Appendix 13.1

Category of Delegated Power	University of Waterloo Act (section 14(1))	Mount Allison University Act	Statutes of Bishop's University	University of Winnipeg Act	University Act (applies to BC universities)
Power to make rules about various matters, including rules and procedures relating to the conduct of its own proceedings			Division 2, Section 1: 1.4 approving the governance rules of the University in keeping with its distinctive characteristics; 1.5 approving the code of ethics applicable to its members and to the members of the University's personnel; 1.7 approving the expertise and experience profiles to be used in appointing its members; 1.10 approving the criteria for evaluating the Board's performance.	may be held, and fixing a quorum.	(x) to make rules consistent with the powers conferred on the board by this Act.

Category of Delegated Power	University of Waterloo Act (section 14(1))	Mount Allison University Act	Statutes of Bishop's University	University of Winnipeg Act	University Act (applies to BC universities)
Power to acquire and govern university property	(c) to plan and implement the physical and operational development of the University and to exercise all the powers to control and achieve a planned rate and scope of such development. (h) to establish and enforce rules and regulations with regard to the use and occupancy of its buildings and grounds or other operations.	4 (e) to receive, purchase, acquire, build upon, hold, possess, enjoy and maintain any property for the use or benefit of the University, without limitation as to the period of holding, and to sell, convey, mortgage, lease or otherwise dispose or any such property. 5 The University shall have a corporate seal and good and valid conveyances or leases of any lands or interests therein may be made by the University under its corporate seal attested	Board of Governors must approve. See 12.2.2 and 12.2.3 above in "Power to enter into agreements."		27 (2) (d) in consultation with the senate, to maintain and keep in proper order and condition the real property of the university, to erect and maintain the buildings and structures on it that in the opinion of the board are necessary and advisable, and to make rules respecting the management, government and control of the real property, buildings and structures. 27 (2) (e) in consultation with the senate, to provide for conservation of the heritage sites of the university, including any heritage

Appendix 13.1

Category of Delegated Power	University of Waterloo Act (section 14(1))	Mount Allison University Act	Statutes of Bishop's University	University of Winnipeg Act	University Act (applies to BC universities)
Power to acquire and govern university property		by the signatures of such officers or other persons as the Board by by-law or otherwise may designate.			buildings, structures and land of the university. 27 2 (t) to regulate, prohibit and impose requirements in relation to the use of real property, buildings, structures and personal property of the university, including in respect of (i) activities and events, (ii) vehicle traffic and parking, including bicycles and other conveyances, and (iii) pedestrian traffic. (t.1) to regulate, prohibit and impose requirements in relation to noise on or in real property, buildings and structures of the university.

Category of Delegated Power	University of Waterloo Act (section 14(1))	Mount Allison University Act	Statutes of Bishop's University	University of Winnipeg Act	University Act (applies to BC universities)
Power to acquire and govern university property					50 (1) For the purposes of carrying out and advancing, directly or indirectly, the purposes of a university, a university may acquire, by gift, purchase or any other manner, and hold, property of any kind. (2) Subject to the approval of the minister and to the terms of any grant, conveyance, gift or devise of land, a university may (a) mortgage, sell, transfer, lease for not more than 99 years, or otherwise dispose of its land, and (b) lease for any term any of its land to a college affiliated with the university.

Appendix 13.1

Category of Delegated Power	University of Waterloo Act (section 14(1))	Mount Allison University Act	Statutes of Bishop's University	University of Winnipeg Act	University Act (applies to BC universities)
Power to enact bylaws	(k) to enact by-laws and regulations for the conduct of its affairs.		Division 2, Section 1: 1.15 making internal management by-laws.		
Power to determine and delegate authority	(j) to provide for the appointment and discharge of committees and for the delegation to and the conferring upon any such committees, authority to act for the Board of Governors with respect to any matter.		Division 2, Section 1: 1.16 determining delegations of authority; 1.19 delegating its powers, in specific cases, to a committee of its members appointed by it.		27 (2) (c) to appoint a secretary and committees it considers necessary to carry out the board's functions, including joint committees with the senate, and to confer on the committees power and authority to act for the board.
Power to grant degrees	Not specified.	4 (c) to grant or to authorize the granting of degrees, honorary degrees, certificates and diplomas.			2 Each university has in its own right and name the power to grant degrees established in accordance with this Act.

Category of Delegated Power	University of Waterloo Act (section 14(1))	Mount Allison University Act	Statutes of Bishop's University	University of Winnipeg Act	University Act (applies to BC universities)
Power with respect to academic organizational structure	Not specified.	4 (b) to establish and maintain such faculties, schools, institutes, departments, chairs and courses as may be desirable.			27 (2) (i) to consider recommendations from the senate for the establishment of faculties and departments with suitable teaching staff and courses of instruction. 27 (2) (j) subject to section 29 and with the approval of the senate, to provide for the establishment of faculties and departments the board considers necessary.
Power to approve strategic plan			Division 2, Section 1: 1.2 approving the strategic directions proposed by the Principal and Vice-Chancellor.		

Appendix 13.1

Category of Delegated Power	University of Waterloo Act (section 14(1))	Mount Allison University Act	Statutes of Bishop's University	University of Winnipeg Act	University Act (applies to BC universities)
Power to approve budget and/or oversee finances			Division 2, Section 1: 1.3 approving the University's budgetary estimates, annual budget, capital plan, financial statements. 1.13 regularly monitoring the University's financial situation and ensuring that the appropriate controls are in place to preserve the University's short-, medium- and long-term financial health.		27 (2) (I) to receive from the president and analyse and adopt with or without modifications the budgets for operating and capital expenditure for the university.

APPENDIX 13.2
A Sample of Powers Delegated to Academic Governing Bodies in Five Pieces of Legislation

Category of Delegated Power	University of Waterloo Act (all references to section 22)[1]	Mount Allison University Act[2]	Statutes of Bishop's University[3]	University of Winnipeg Act[4]	University Act (applies to BC universities)[5]
Name of governing body	Senate	Senate	Senate	Senate	Senate
General academic governance	22. The Senate has the power to establish the educational policies of the University and to make recommendations to the Board of Governors with respect to any matter relative to	17 (5) The Senate shall have the following functions, powers and duties: (c) to regulate in general all other matters relating to academic departments of the University, subject always to the	Division 1 — Section 1.1: The Board of Governors shall respect the responsibility of the University Senate to adopt policies on academic matters, subject to the approval of the Board of Governors.	24 (1) The senate is responsible for the academic policy of the university. Subject to the oversight and approval of the Board of Governors, the powers and	37 (1) The academic governance of the university is vested in the senate and it has the following powers: 37 (1) (y) to do and perform all other matters and things that

1 https://uwaterloo.ca/secretariat/governance/university-waterloo-act#Powers-of-Board-of-Governors.
2 www.mta.ca/Community/Governance_and_admin/Governance/Board_of_Regents/Mount_Allison_University_Act/Mount_Allison_University_Act.
3 www.ubishops.ca/wp-content/uploads/200501_Statutes-Bishops-University-approved-by-the-Board-of-Governors.pdf.
4 www.uwinnipeg.ca/regents/uofw-act.pdf.
5 www.bclaws.gov.bc.ca/civix/document/id/complete/statreg/96468_01.

Appendix 13.2

Category of Delegated Power	University of Waterloo Act (section 14(1))	Mount Allison University Act	Statutes of Bishop's University	University of Winnipeg Act	University Act (applies to BC universities)
General academic governance	the operation of the University and without restricting the generality of the foregoing, this includes the power	powers delegated to the President by subsection 13(3). 17 (5) (e) to exercise such other functions, powers and duties as may from time to time be conferred upon it by the Board.	Responsibilities of the Senate shall be as follows: Division 1 – 5.4.1 to govern the academic work and life of the University.	24 (2) (k) deal with any other matters of an academic nature.	may be necessary or advisable for carrying out and advancing, directly or indirectly, the purposes of the university and the performance of any duty by the board or its officers prescribed by this Act or the *Sexual Violence and Misconduct Policy Act*.
Powers with respect to academic organization structure		(a) to make recommendations to the Board of Governors relative to the creation, establishment, maintenance, modification, or removal of organizational structures such as faculties, schools, institutes, departments or chairs within the University.	Division 1 – 5.4.2 to prepare and recommend plans and policies for the academic development of the University, including by way of example, the following: – areas of study; – organization of academic activities (such as faculties,	24 (2) (i) consider and make recommendation to the board concerning (i) changes in the composition of faculties, schools, departments, chairs and programs of study, (ii) major changes to the academic and research programs of the university in light	37 (1) (i) to recommend to the board the establishment or discontinuance of any faculty, department, course of instruction.

Category of Delegated Power	University of Waterloo Act (section 14(1))	Mount Allison University Act	Statutes of Bishop's University	University of Winnipeg Act	University Act (applies to BC universities)
Powers with respect to academic organization structure			schools, divisions, programs and departments); – graduate studies policy; – methods of teaching and study; – educational standards; – library and other academic services; – conduct of examinations; – recommending to Convocation the granting of all degrees in course; – nature of all scholarships, fellowships and awards; – admissions; and – size and composition of faculty.	of available financial resources, (iii) affiliations with other academic institutions, and (iv) any other matter the senate considers appropriate.	

Appendix 13.2

Category of Delegated Power	University of Waterloo Act (section 14(1))	Mount Allison University Act	Statutes of Bishop's University	University of Winnipeg Act	University Act (applies to BC universities)
Powers over academic programming and courses of study	(b) subject to the approval of the Board of Governors, in so far as the expenditure of funds is concerned, to establish, maintain, modify or remove, curricula of all courses of instruction including extension courses.		See 5.4.2. above. Division 1 – Section 5.12: Courses and Terms of Study – The courses of study shall consist of such academic requirements and subjects as are prescribed by the Senate. The period allotted to study in each year shall be divided into terms, the opening and closing dates of which are in each case determined by the Senate.	24(2)(b) consider and determine all courses and programs of study, including requirements and procedures for admission, examination and graduation.	37 (1) (f) to consider, approve and recommend to the board the revision of courses of study, instruction and education in all faculties and departments of the university. (g) to provide for courses of study in any place in British Columbia and to encourage and develop extension and correspondence programs.

Category of Delegated Power	University of Waterloo Act (section 14(1))	Mount Allison University Act	Statutes of Bishop's University	University of Winnipeg Act	University Act (applies to BC universities)
Powers with respect to faculty appointments and promotions (either authority to appoint or to approve the policies governing appointment)	(c) to determine policies concerning the qualifications of faculty members within the University with respect to appointments or promotions in rank, or to the granting of tenure, in connection with research or teaching or academic administration.			(i) consider and make recommendation to the board concerning (i) changes in the composition of faculties, schools, departments, chairs and programs of study.	37 (1) (k) to determine the members of the teaching and administrative staffs who are to be members of each faculty.
Powers with respect to admission policies and standards	(d) to determine standards of admission of students to the University.	17 (5) (a) to determine the requisites for admission and the courses of study for graduates and undergraduates.	See 5.4.2, above Division 1 — Section 6.9: Admission — Candidates shall be admitted to degrees by the Chancellor according to norms established from time to time by Senate and published in the University Calendar; they shall	See 24(2)(b).	37 (1) (c) to determine all questions relating to the academic and other qualifications required of applicants for admission as students to the university or to any faculty, and to determine in which faculty the students pursuing a course of study must register.

Appendix 13.2 151

Category of Delegated Power	University of Waterloo Act (section 14(1))	Mount Allison University Act	Statutes of Bishop's University	University of Winnipeg Act	University Act (applies to BC universities)
Powers with respect to admission policies and standards			receive written evidence of their admission to these degrees.		
Powers with respect to examinations policies and standards	(e) to consider and determine the conduct and results of examinations in all faculties or academic units.		See 5.4.2, above. Division 1 – Section 5.13: Examinations and Graduation – All matters dealing with examinations and graduation shall be determined from time to time by the Senate, which shall cause the appropriate announcements to be published in the University Calendar.	See 24(2)(b).	37 (1) (d) to determine the conditions under which candidates must be received for examination, to appoint examiners and to determine the conduct and results of all examinations. 37 (1) (r) subject to the approval of the board, to enter into agreements with any corporation or society in British Columbia entitled under any Act to establish examinations for admission to the corporation

Category of Delegated Power	University of Waterloo Act (section 14(1))	Mount Allison University Act	Statutes of Bishop's University	University of Winnipeg Act	University Act (applies to BC universities)
Powers with respect to examinations policies and standards					or society, for the purpose of conducting examinations and reporting results, and those corporations or societies have power to enter into the agreements.

37 (1) (s) to make rules respecting the conduct and financing of examinations referred to in paragraph (r) and other examinations conducted by the senate under any other Act.

37 (1) (t) to make rules respecting the reporting of results of examinations referred to in paragraphs (r) and (s). |

Appendix 13.2 153

Category of Delegated Power	University of Waterloo Act (section 14(1))	Mount Allison University Act	Statutes of Bishop's University	University of Winnipeg Act	University Act (applies to BC universities)
Powers with respect to discipline for student academic or other misconduct, and appeals from the same	(f) to hear and determine appeals from the decisions of the faculty councils on applications and examinations by students.			24 (2) (d.1) exercise internal disciplinary jurisdiction over the academic conduct of students, including the power to expel or suspend for cause. 24 (2) (h) hear and determine any appeals by students concerning their academic standing that the senate considers appropriate.	37 (1) (v) to establish a standing committee of final appeal for students in matters of academic discipline.
Degree-granting powers	(g) to confer degrees, diplomas and certificates or other awards in any and all branches of learning and in any subject taught in the University or its federated or affiliated colleges.	17 (5) (b) to examine the qualifications of all candidates for degrees and authorize the conferring of degrees on properly qualified persons.	See 5.4.2, above Division 1 – Section 6.2: Degrees – All degrees which it is in the power of the University to grant shall be conferred by Convocation.	24 (2) (c) determine the degrees, including honorary degrees, diplomas and certificates of proficiency to be granted by the university, and the persons to whom they are to be granted and the	37 (1) (h) to provide for and to grant degrees, including honorary degrees, diplomas and certificates of proficiency, except in theology.

Category of Delegated Power	University of Waterloo Act (section 14(1))	Mount Allison University Act	Statutes of Bishop's University	University of Winnipeg Act	University Act (applies to BC universities)
Degree-granting powers	(h) to confer honorary degrees in Divinity, without fees, upon the recommendation of any theological college federated or affiliated with the University. (i) to confer honorary degrees in any department of learning.		6.2.1 Degrees in course shall be granted on the recommendation of the Senate. 6.2.2 Degrees honoris causa shall be granted on the recommendation of the Degree Committee.	persons to be admitted as fellows.	
Financial, resource, or other budgetary advisory responsibility	(k) to consider and to recommend to the Board of Governors policies concerning the internal allocation or use of University resources.			24 (2) (e) directly and through its committees, request and receive from the board and from the administrative staff of the university, any fiscal and other information that in the senate's opinion may be needed to enable it to carry out its responsibilities.	37 (1) (e) to establish a standing committee to meet with the president and assist the president in preparing the university budget.

Appendix 13.2

Category of Delegated Power	University of Waterloo Act (section 14(1))	Mount Allison University Act	Statutes of Bishop's University	University of Winnipeg Act	University Act (applies to BC universities)
Financial, resource, or other budgetary advisory responsibility				24 (2) (i) consider and make recommendation to the board concerning ... (ii) major changes to the academic and research programs of the university in light of available financial resources.	
Powers respecting affiliation of the university with other institutions and the governance of the same	(l) to consider and to recommend to the Board of Governors the federation or affiliation of the University with any college for teaching any branch of learning.		Division 1 — Section 5.15: Affiliation — Colleges and Schools which fulfil adequate conditions of teaching and control may be affiliated to the University by action of the Board of Governors under such terms and conditions as the Senate may prescribe.	24 (2) (i) consider and make recommendation to the board concerning ... (iii) affiliations with other academic institutions.	37 (1) (u) to set the terms of affiliation with other universities, colleges or other institutions of learning, and to modify or terminate the affiliation.

Category of Delegated Power	University of Waterloo Act (section 14(1))	Mount Allison University Act	Statutes of Bishop's University	University of Winnipeg Act	University Act (applies to BC universities)
Powers to establish policies, bylaws, and rules for the conduct of its own affairs/ governance	(m) to create councils and committees to exercise its powers. (n) to provide, if considered necessary, for an executive committee which shall act in the name and on behalf of the Senate between regular meetings of the Senate. (o) to enact by-laws and regulations for the conduct of its affairs.		Division 1 — Section 11.4: Policies and Procedures — The Board of Governors, the Senate, Bishop's Council, Faculty Council, Staff Council, Managers' Council and any of their respective committees may establish their own internal policies and procedures which shall be supplementary, but not contradictory, to those contained in these Statutes.	24 (2) Without limiting subsection (1), the senate may (a) establish rules and procedures for the conduct of its proceedings, including fixing a quorum. 24 (2) (j) appoint any standing and other committees that it considers necessary. 24 (2) (g) make regulations respecting the activities of faculty members and students as they affect the academic life of the university.	37 (1) (a) to regulate the conduct of its meetings and proceedings, including the determination of the quorum necessary for the transaction of its business, and the election of a vice-chair at least annually, who is to chair meetings in the absence of the president. 37 (1) (b) to establish committees it considers necessary and, by 2/3 vote of its members present, to delegate to one or more committees those of its powers as it may determine.

Category of Delegated Power	University of Waterloo Act (section 14(1))	Mount Allison University Act	Statutes of Bishop's University	University of Winnipeg Act	University Act (applies to BC universities)
Powers to establish policies, bylaws, and rules for the conduct of its own affairs/ governance					37 (1) (q) to establish a standing committee to consider and take action on behalf of the senate on all matters that may be referred to the senate by the board. 37 (1) (x) to make rules consistent with the powers conferred on the board by this Act.
Powers with respect to awards, scholarships and bursaries			See 5.4.2, above.	24 (2) (d) award scholarships, bursaries, medals and prizes.	37 (1) (i) to recommend to the board the establishment or discontinuance of any . . . fellowship, scholarship, exhibition, bursary or prize. 37 (1) (j) to award fellowships, scholarships, exhibitions, bursaries and prizes.

Category of Delegated Power	University of Waterloo Act (section 14(1))	Mount Allison University Act	Statutes of Bishop's University	University of Winnipeg Act	University Act (applies to BC universities)
Delegation of responsibility to give recommendations or advice on a wide variety of matters to the governing board or others	(j) to undertake, consider and co-ordinate long-range academic planning.	15 (5) (d) to make recommendations to the Board on any matter of interest to the University.	Division 1 - Section 4.2.1: The Principal and Vice-Chancellor, the Vice-Principal Academic, the Vice-Principal Finance and Administration, the Dean of Student Affairs, the Secretary General and the University Librarian shall be appointed by the Board of Governors after consultation with the Senate.	24(2)(f) carry out any responsibilities concerning contractual and other matters assigned to it by the board.	37 (1) (o) to make recommendations to the board considered advisable for promoting the interests of the university or for carrying out the objects and provisions of this Act.

CHAPTER 14

Shared Governance

A. THE PARAMETERS OF SHARED GOVERNANCE

In Chapter 11, I described bicameral governance generally, noting that in Canada, we also have examples of unicameral and tricameral governance models. Your university legislation establishes the specific parameters of governance at your institution because it establishes the roles, powers, and obligations of the governance bodies. We're now focusing on the relationship between the board and the academic governing body. The following general principles are likely true:

1) Your legislation establishes the board and sets out its powers and responsibilities.
2) Your legislation establishes your academic governing body and sets out its powers and responsibilities.
3) The relationship between the board and the academic governing body will have four main facets:
   i. The board will have its own set of powers and duties.
   ii. The academic governing body will have its own set of powers and duties. (There are examples of universities in which the legislation provides that the academic governing body is advisory in nature.)[1]

---

1   See, for example, *The University of Ontario Institute of Technology Act, 2002*, S.O. 2002, c. 8, Schedule O. Note, however, that in this instance the powers of the governing body

iii. There may be powers and duties shared between the board and the academic governing body. The British Columbia *University Act* provides for a sharing of powers between the senate and board for the establishment of faculties and departments.[2] In other words, the board can establish faculties and departments, but only with the approval of the academic governing body.
iv. The board may be required to consult with the academic governing body before deciding a matter. Under the *University of Winnipeg Act*, the board may authorize affiliations with other academic institutions if the senate recommends it, or if the board wishes to authorize it after consulting with the senate.[3]

It is important to point out again that the roles of the governing bodies at different institutions are unique to the institution. Note, for example, the difference between the general statements of power of the senate at Bishop's University and the University of Waterloo.

University Legislation	Bishop's University	University of Waterloo
General Statement	Subject to the oversight and approval of the Board of Governors, the powers and responsibilities of the Senate shall be as follows.	The Senate has the power to establish the educational policies of the University.

In Bishop's University's statement, the legislation provides that all of the work of the senate is subject to board oversight and approval. The University of Waterloo legislation does not subject the senate's exercise of its powers to board oversight. Note that in practice, the two statements may be applied similarly, and Bishop's board of governors may, as a matter of practice, defer to the decisions of the senate and very rarely exercise oversight. As you read your legislation and bylaws, ask yourself about the legislative and practical relationships between the board and the academic governing body.

---

are delegated through bylaws. See Article 1 of The University of Ontario Institute of Technology, By-law No 2-2018, online: https://shared.ontariotechu.ca/shared/department/opp/Governance/uoit-by-law/final-approved-by-law-no-2-website-version.pdf.
2   *University Act*, RSBC 1996, c 468.
3   *University of Winnipeg Act*, CCSM c U70.

There is no clear line between the work of the academic governing body and the board. An example given by the former president of two Canadian universities, Ross Paul, illustrates this:

> [T]he senate's authority to set admission standards has significant implications for enrolments and hence for the financial position of the institution, and there is little point in approving an academic program if there is not a good market case for it and the requisite funding. It is thus imperative that boards and senates function effectively together with good communications and mutual respect.[4]

It is the university governance professional's role to steer the governing bodies through decision-making paths and navigate the way of shared delegation and responsibility. As Paul's example shows, governance is ineffective if the bodies operate in isolation. It cannot be the case that one governing body makes a decision, indifferent as to the effect of the decision on the other body. As a board member, it is important that you understand the authority of your institution's academic governing body, the areas of potential conflict, and the areas in which the board has the obligation to consult or involve your academic governing body.

B. CHALLENGES RAISED BY THE ISSUES OF ACADEMIC GOVERNING BODY EFFECTIVENESS

It is my observation that university board governance is increasingly sophisticated, although there is still a very long way to go. Academic governing bodies, by their own members' estimation, are not effective (see the work done by Pennock et al, below). Academic governing bodies play a critical role in university governance, and if they are not effective, a key aspect of the university's governance is ineffective. In describing the role of the board, I urged board members to understand that effective governance underpins their ability to defend institutional autonomy. This part of the chapter gives you a bit more insight into the barriers to effective governance within your institution. There are two key issues to address: (1) combatting the erosion of academic governing body power and effectiveness by faculty unions, and (2) combatting perceptions on the part of academic governing body members that their governing bodies are ineffective.

---

4   Ross Paul, *Leadership Under Fire: The Challenging Role of the Canadian University President* (Quebec: McGill-Queen's University Press, 2011) at 195.

C. THE EFFECT OF FACULTY UNIONS UPON ACADEMIC GOVERNING BODIES

In Chapter 11, in the context of the discussion about bicameralism, I alerted you to concerns about the effect of unionization on governance generally. The CAUT encourages its faculty association members to get involved in governance at their universities. It's important for boards to have a sense of faculty perspective, and I say this from the point of view of one who observes as external board members try to understand faculty, and who sees the miscommunication that results from two parties with fundamentally different outlooks.

In his book *More Than an Academic Question: Universities, Government and Public Policy in Canada*, David Cameron traced the roots of faculty unionization in Canada. There are two aspects of the faculty perspective that boards should understand: (1) the continuing belief that faculty should be self-governing, and (2) the concept that faculty are not employees of the university, but are, rather, members. Cameron states that faculty start from the position that "the only proper conception of the university [is] a community of scholars, ideally governed by its members."[5] If this is the starting point for faculty, one can see how the bicameral model, with a board overseeing a "public corporation," is a continuing source of disappointment that drives various attempts to change the system. As mentioned in Chapter 6, faculty are key stakeholders and partners in governance through their roles on the board and on the academic governing body. Understanding the (sometimes conflicting) views of faculty, on themselves as members and not employees of the institution, on faculty self-governance and unionization, is important for board members.

1) Faculty Self-Government and Increased Participation in University Governance

Faculty associations and CAUT have tried for many years to move universities closer to a model of faculty self-government. A 1955 survey (Rowat) revealed that some senates were dominated by non-academic members and worse, the governing legislation prohibited faculty and staff from sitting on

---

5 David M Cameron, *More Than an Academic Question: Universities, Government and Public Policy in Canada* (Halifax: The Institute for Research on Public Policy, 1991) at 343.

the governing boards.⁶ This caused Rowat several concerns, including the concern that "faculty came to be treated as employees of the board rather than as full members of the university."⁷ Rowat recommended changes to the governing board model to increase the proportion of faculty on the board to 50 percent.

In 1957, CAUT took up the cause of increasing faculty involvement on the governing board. Reform was advanced from several quarters, and by 1964 the Duff-Berdahl Commission was formed to study the matter. The commissioners supported bicameralism, but found that Canadian bicameralism had several flaws: senates were ineffective because they were too large and had too many non-academic members; the role of senates should be expanded to include academic planning; senates should advise and make recommendations to boards; and governing boards, "while retaining ultimate legal and financial authority, should be more broadly representative of the wider community and ... should include [up to 25 percent] faculty members elected by and from the reformed senate."⁸

Duff-Berdahl proposed a number of other reforms, including faculty involvement in senior administrator selection, and limited term appointments for academic administrators, among others. To say that the Duff-Berdahl report was influential is an understatement. Its recommendations caused significant change in university governance across the country. One unanticipated effect was that students demanded representation on university boards too, and were successful in securing it. In 1955, faculty members were on 9 percent of Canadian boards, and no boards had student members. By 1975, 92 percent of Canadian university boards had faculty as members, and 78 percent had student members.⁹ On senates, faculty and administrative members lost a little ground to students: in 1965, administrative officers made up 27 percent, faculty members 55 percent, and others (not including students) the remaining 18 percent of senate members. By 1975, administrative members made up 26 percent, faculty members 53 percent, students 14 percent, and others 7 percent of senate members.¹⁰

---

6   *Ibid* at 299.
7   *Ibid* at 300.
8   *Ibid* at 306.
9   *Ibid* at 314.
10 *Ibid* at 316.

2) Unionization

CAUT was established in 1951, and at that time, seven universities had unionized faculty.[11] By the mid-1950s, the number had doubled.[12] Some within academe realized that unionization was at odds with the concept of faculty self-governance and membership (rather than employment) in an institution, and as Cameron describes it, the 1960s were a decade-long period of debate.[13] One opponent recognized the contradictions inherent in self-governing community members seeking to unionize:

> The creation of a viable trade union structure for Canadian universities would … involve far-reaching changes in the atmosphere of the university, which would no longer be that of a community of scholars, but that of a factory.[14]

Increasing unionization in the United States, market conditions, and provincial legislation contributed to the growth of faculty unionization.[15] The 1972 Adell-Carter study predicted multiple effects of faculty unionizations, and these predictions were remarkably prescient and accurate (as those working in governance in Canadian universities will recognize). The first effect was that of "'creeping legalism': a system in which the attitudes of the most nitpicking and legalistic individuals in the university become the dominant attitudes."[16] The study went on to note that: "[c]reeping legalism is unfortunately inherent in the adversary [sic] nature of the collective bargaining relationship, and can be kept under control only by constant use of common sense on both sides."[17] Adell and Carter further predicted "an inevitable conflict in faculty roles, resulting from the juxtaposition of collective bargaining and participatory management. Faculty members, they argued, "want both the right to participate in the running of their universities and the right to confront as adversaries the people who set their terms and conditions of employment. That there is a logical inconsistency here is beyond doubt."[18] It is important for members of boards and academic

---

11   *Ibid* at 345.
12   *Ibid*.
13   *Ibid* at 349.
14   *Ibid* at 346.
15   *Ibid* at 344–50.
16   *Ibid* at 350–51.
17   *Ibid* at 351.
18   *Ibid*.

governing bodies to understand that union participation in governance undermines good governance. Unions cannot effectively serve their own interests and those of their members, and also purport to objectively act in the best interests of the institution and all of its stakeholders.

The reality that universities and their governing bodies must address today is one in which unionization is a dominant force and in which the explicit agenda of CAUT is to negotiate provisions within the collective agreement that will govern the operation of the board and academic governing body.[19] CAUT has concluded that senates are not "reliable and consistent vehicles through which academic staff can ensure their proper role in the academic governance of their institutions" and thus CAUT states that "[w]e believe that academic staff associations must turn to collective bargaining to ensure their position in academic decision-making as part of their terms and conditions of employment."[20] The interference by unions undermines good governance, and in turn, weakened governance gives unions fodder to argue that they must step in to fill the gaps in governance. Universities must counteract the weakening of governance by strengthening and enlivening their academic governing bodies to allow the engaged and widespread involvement of individual faculty members (not their unions or union leaders) in academic governance.

It is interesting to note that the majority of academic governing board members do not see the value of union involvement in matters belonging to the academic governing body. Pennock et al observe "ambivalence about the role of faculty unions," with 41 percent of senate members disagreeing with the statement: "The role of our senate has been strengthened by the work of the faculty association/union."[21] The authors go on to state that "[i]t does not appear that most sitting senate members are looking to their bargaining units to supplant the collegial governance model."[22] This is good news for university governance, and ultimately for the preservation of a governance model that supports university autonomy.

---

19   "CAUT Policy Statement," Canadian Association of University Teachers (November 2019), online: CAUT www.caut.ca/about-us/caut-policy/lists/caut-policy-statements/policy-statement-on-governance at point 4.
20   Lea Pennock et al, "Challenges and Opportunities for Collegial Governance at Canadian Universities: Reflections on a Survey of Academic Senates" (2016) 46 *Canadian Journal of Higher Education* 73 at 83.
21   Ibid.
22   Ibid.

The power of the collective bargaining interest on the governing bodies effectively leaves the university working with two "representatives" of academic interests within the institution: faculty unions and the academic governing body. The board must resist the attempts to further blur the line between the purview of faculty associations that negotiate the terms and conditions of faculty employment, and the purview of the academic governing bodies that oversee academic governance. I've quoted scholars who have said this a number of ways, and will finish by noting that the Duff-Berdahl commissioners also cautioned against the intended role of the senate being usurped by the faculty association, "a body of protest rather than of achievement,"[23] and by referring again to Peter MacKinnon. He advises that bicameral governance (and thus university autonomy) is under threat, and that a significant aspect of the threat is

> the encroachment of faculty unions upon the domain of boards and senates. Faculty unions are mandated to protect and advance the employment interests of their members; they are not mandated to co-manage universities or to displace and diminish the authority of their governing bodies. The legal and cultural norms of trade unionism, imported from industrial organization into the public sector, including most Canadian universities, are not compatible with a broader role in their management or governance. Moreover, faculty union and CAUT initiatives to diminish senates . . . invite intervention from governments if university administrations are unsuccessful in resisting them.[24]

If the academic governing body lacks the vigour to defend itself against incursions by other interests, and waives the opportunity to engage in partnership with the board, this is a failure of governance, with the risk of further loss of institutional autonomy.

D. INCREASING ACADEMIC GOVERNING BODY EFFECTIVENESS

It continues to be the case today that academic governing bodies are less effective than they need to be to engage fully in the governance work of the institution. Glen Jones reports that 65 percent of governing members

---

23   Cameron, above note 5 at 306.
24   Peter MacKinnon, *University Leadership and Public Policy in the Twenty-First Century: A President's Perspective* (Toronto: University of Toronto Press, 2014) at 157.

believe that their body is an important forum for discussion, but only 44 percent of them think that they are effective.[25] There has not been a lot of academic work done on Canadian academic governing bodies, but thanks to Dr. Jones and a number of academic colleagues across the country, we have the results of some informative studies. One study from 2016 (built on previous studies) identified suggestions for reform. Pennock et al are encouraging, as they note that there is survey information that shows members of senates feel they are more effective now than they were ten years ago. The authors suggest hopefully that "senates in Canada are not in peril."[26] Their suggestions for reform are helpful and I support them. Pennock et al suggest that senates should

1) focus on their own performance;
2) focus on the academic performance ...;
3) adopt corporate governance practices that serve the senate's mission.[27]

Focusing on performance (the first two recommendations) will lead to "more appropriate ... meetings."[28] While academic governing bodies may not want to embrace holus-bolus private-sector practices, their ends are worthwhile cultivating: productive meetings, transparent decision-making, timely identification and mitigation of risk, robust performance measurement, due diligence and an informed governing body.[29]

University boards and senior administrators can support effective governance by maintaining a focus on the specific roles of the board, the academic governing body, and the administration. Boards have a responsibility to improve communication and the relationship between the governing bodies. Finally, as addressed in the next chapter, the president, who often is also the chair of the academic governing body has a key role in fostering the right culture and strategic focus.

E. THE VITAL ROLE OF THE GOVERNANCE PROFESSIONAL

The vital role of governance professionals within institutions is overlooked and undervalued; many institutions still hire individuals on the basis of

---

25 Glen A Jones, "Trends in Academic Governance in Canada," University of Toronto (28 January 2020), online: www.slideplayer.com/slide/6675800.
26 Pennock et al, above note 13 at 83–84.
27 *Ibid* at 84.
28 *Ibid*.
29 *Ibid*.

the expectation that the governing body secretaries will take minutes and organize workflow. Universities that fail to appreciate that governance is a discipline miss the opportunity to hire individuals who understand the strategic importance of effective governance and who can have a positive effect on governance itself. I am a supporter of the secretariats for the academic governing body and the governing board being combined. This organization enables significant efficiencies, and promotes communication, complementary processes, and governance goals. It also enables the identification of opportunities for collaboration and cooperation between the governing bodies. Where the two bodies are separate, all possible measures should be taken to ensure seamless communication and cooperation. All of this is necessary for effective governance.

F. CONCLUSION

Effective shared governance is foundational to institutional autonomy. This chapter attempts to help board members understand some of the threats to effective shared governance and to encourage focus on measures to combat these threats. Boards, academic governing bodies, administrative leaders, and governance professionals all have a role to play. Faculty associations also have a role to play in recognizing the conflict inherent in their attempts to replace collegial governance with union participation in governance. Faculty associations can support good governance by encouraging their members to participate in governance as independent actors with a commitment to governing in the best interests of the university and all of its stakeholders.

CHAPTER 15

The Board and the President

The importance of the relationship between the board and the president cannot be understated. One of the board's main tasks involves the hiring, management, support, and, if necessary, termination of the president. The presidential hiring process is long and very public, with the consequence that a poor decision is financially costly. More importantly, a failed presidency represents a huge opportunity cost and a major community relations issue for the board. And, university presidencies in Canada really do fail at a rate of about 20 percent.[1] What, then, can the board do to ensure that it hires the right president and helps that person to succeed?[2]

---

1   Anna Stuart, Ross Paul & Peter George, "Leadership in Academia: Onboarding," Knightsbridge Robertson Surrette (2012), online: KBRS www.kbrs.ca/insights/leadership-academia-onboarding. The authors state that "[a]n estimated 20% of recent presidential appointments among Canadian universities were unsuccessful, resulting in the president either leaving before the end of the first term or failing to meet the expectations and objectives set out for them."

2   For specific "Smart Practice" tips, see Karen E Hakkarainen, "A Smart Practice Guide to Presidential Transition: A Resource for Governing Boards and New Presidents of Canadian Public Universities" (June 2018), online: https://dspace.library.uvic.ca:8443/handle/1828/10561.

A. THE CHALLENGE OF THE PRESIDENTIAL ROLE

The first thing that a university board has to understand is that the role of university president is a very difficult one. Ross Paul, a former university president, wrote a lengthy book, aptly called *Leadership Under Fire*, on this very challenging role.[3] It describes in the following terms the broad scope of the role of the Canadian university president and what that person has to do for a wide variety of stakeholders:

- The faculty want an academic leader who will bring visibility, reputation, and prestige to the institution, someone who strongly defends academic freedom and finds as much money as possible for teaching and research.
- The board wants a strong leader with excellent management, communication, and human relations skills, a good fundraiser and promoter, a leader of unquestioned integrity and strength who ensures the financial stability of the institution.
- Students want an informal role model who is actively engaged on campus, highly accessible, and particularly sensitive to such concerns as support services, teaching and learning, and affordable tuition fees.
- Alumni want a highly visible and personable representative of the institution who actively supports their activities and intercollegiate sports, and who is both knowledgeable about and appreciative of the institution's history and culture.
- The local community wants a high-profile promoter of the institution and its environs who is approachable.
- The governments want individuals who can initiate and manage change, who know how to work within the academic culture, understand the fiscal challenges, are openly accountable for the use of public moneys, and help realize public policy priorities through leadership of their respective institutions.[4]

A prominent academic executive recruiter in Canada echoes some of the above and observes that for university presidents, there are "three key leadership competencies that are essential for success in leading today's

---

3   Ross Paul, *Leadership Under Fire: The Challenging Role of the Canadian University President* (Quebec: McGill-Queen's University Press, 2011).
4   *Ibid* at 12–13.

university—relationship management, influence and persuasion and resilience."⁵ As Peter MacKinnon notes:

> The unique governance and collegial management of universities means that their presidents do not have the same powers [as corporate CEOs,] a fact not always understood by those outside the university, [nor by] some ... within, who look to the president for many things, including accountability for results ..., [but] presidents increasingly are held to account for results over which they have little control.⁶

MacKinnon goes on to describe how metrics-based performance measurement and increasing accountability for university performance put extreme pressure on presidents who do not have corresponding levels of control over the institutions they are supposed to change.

Why don't presidents have more control? Earlier chapters have discussed the complexity of universities: dispersed power, territoriality, effects of unionization, shared governance, university politics, the interventions of governments and other external stakeholders, and academic freedom. There's more: described by MacKinnon as "collegial management," others have called it "democratic management."⁷ As described in Chapter 14, boards and academic governing bodies changed in the 1970s to include many more faculty members, and students. They became, in a sense, more "democratic." In a further broadening of the concept, this democratic management includes two other principles: (1) faculty committees should be involved in "decisions on appointments, reappointment, promotion, etc.,"⁸ and (2) "[a]cademic administrators, from the departmental level to the presidency, should be appointed for fixed terms and after consultation with, if not election by, the faculty members concerned."⁹ Collegial management effectively means that faculty have significant influence, if not control, over academic human resources decisions. While the president's role is to run the university and to be answerable for the performance of those working within the university, the board must understand that

---

5   Anna Stuart, "What Is Leadership," Knightsbridge Robertson Surrette (February 2013), online: KBRS www.kbrs.ca/sites/default/files/viewpoint_feb.pdf.
6   Peter MacKinnon, *University Leadership and Public Policy in the Twenty-First Century: A President's Perspective* (Toronto: University of Toronto Press, 2014) at 134–35.
7   David M Cameron, *More Than an Academic Question: Universities, Government and Public Policy in Canada* (Halifax: The Institute for Research on Public Policy, 1991) at 313.
8   *Ibid* at 316.
9   *Ibid* at 317.

this faculty influence and power dilutes, and in some cases, removes the president's control over human resources decisions in hiring, tenure and promotion (among others). Again, the theme of obligation without control.

B. LAYING THE FOUNDATION FOR A NEW PRESIDENT TO SUCCEED

Hiring the right president is the board's "single most important task."[10] While many things are out of the board's control, there are some things a board can do to increase its chances of success in hiring the right president.

1) Understand the University's Culture

The end of a president's tenure presents an opportunity for positive change. This is true even if the departing president made positive progress as a leader. However, the board must be careful that the change it envisions is one the institution is capable of. This is a difficult assessment, but if the board ensures that its aspirations for change are grounded in careful assessment of the university's current capacity and tolerance for change, the new president has a better chance of meeting the board's expectations. What does that mean? Well, knowing that universities are difficult to manage, and knowing that change is difficult in much less complex environments, the board must build on existing elements of university culture and identity. Ross Paul states that university presidents who come to universities with grand and dramatic plans for change "seldom succeed."[11] He advises presidents to approach change carefully and to "start with the issue(s) the organization faces, refocus the agenda, use the considerable extant change knowledge and then shape and leverage the strength of existing cultures and leaders."[12] Boards should take heed when they undertake the search for a new president, and should avoid setting unrealistic objectives.

2) Understand University Expectations Related to Presidential Recruitment

Boards can lay the foundation of success for a new president by following a sound recruitment process. This may seem trite, but what is sound elsewhere

---

10   MacKinnon, above note 6 at 139.
11   Paul, above note 3 at 71.
12   *Ibid.*

does not apply in the context of universities. Recruiting a new president is a significant undertaking, and as the role has become more challenging, "the number of traditionally qualified, interested candidates has declined."[13] New board members are often surprised by, and resistant to, the nature of the process universities follow to recruit presidents. In keeping with principles of democratic management, the process to hire a new president, while run by the board, is a process that involves the university community. The process is much longer and more transparent than in the private sector, and it involves extensive community consultation. In my experience, twelve to eighteen months is a good estimate of the amount of time it takes for the key steps in the presidential search process. As you've heard many times before, each university follows different practices, but the search generally includes the following:

- broad community consultation
- the formation of a search committee
- selection and engagement of a search consultant
- development of an extensive candidate profile and brief
- shortlisting, interviewing, and selection of the candidate

The university community expects that the consultation process undertaken in the context of a presidential search will be designed to engage the university's stakeholders to provide feedback on the community's view of the president's strategic priorities, or of the skills and attributes necessary to meet the universities' strategic priorities. This is an important process that will inform the board as to what the community believes are the important challenges facing the university and to get a sense of the type of person the community is seeking. The community will expect the process to be transparent and accessible, and this means that the board should ensure that the community can participate in different ways (for example, in town halls, focus groups, surveys). The hiring of a new president is also an opportunity for the board to engage external stakeholders, such as government and industry leaders, about the role of the university in the community.

Again we see principles of democratic management at play in the formation and role of the search committee. The committee itself is advisory to the board and includes different stakeholders (at a minimum board members, faculty, staff, and students). While the role of the search committee

---

13 Anna Stuart, "The Case for Change: Reimagining the Academic Leadership Search Process," Knightsbridge Robertson Surrette (n.d.), online: KBRS www.kbrs.ca/insights/case-change-reimagining-academic-leadership-search-process.

will vary, generally the search committee will be involved in some or all of the following tasks: selecting the search consultant; the community consultation process; developing the candidate brief; and shortlisting, interviewing, and recommending the final candidate or candidates (depending on the process) to the board for appointment.

This first step in the recruitment process sets the foundation for the success of your new university president. It is crucial that your university communities feel engaged and consulted with from the start and that they can see their perspectives reflected in the job posting and the candidate brief. There are always concerns and complaints about the nature and breadth of community consultation and engagement. It is essential to the new president's legitimacy and acceptance by the community that the board runs a good, consistent process with effective community consultation and communication throughout. Board members from outside the sector may be impatient with the process when they compare it to the relative ease with which senior leadership hiring decisions are made in the private sector, but take shortcuts at the peril of the board and the new president!

As board members are often surprised by the length of time presidential searches take, it's worthwhile making a note about timing. Conducting a search process through a committee means allowing for more time. Given the size of the committees, scheduling can be challenging. Both the search consultant and the search committee chair play an important, challenging, and crucial role in facilitating decisions to conclusion. Most often, academic appointments in Canada are effective at the beginning of the academic year, which is 1 July across the country. Your new president, then, if coming from a Canadian academic role, will start on that date. Search activities are generally planned backward from 1 July, which is the common start date for a new president.

It is the board's role to set and conclude the negotiations of the terms and conditions of the president's employment, although in some provinces, provincial legislation constrains what can be included in the president's offer. In Ontario, for example, public-sector accountability and executive compensation legislation have been in place for many years, and compensation has effectively been frozen for Ontario higher-education executives for about ten years.[14]

---

14 "Broader Public Sector Accountability," Government of Ontario (26 August 2015), online: Government of Ontario www.ontario.ca/page/broader-public-sector-accountability.

Considerations of equity, diversity, and inclusion are not to be forgotten through the presidential search process. A good search consultant will assist the board in this regard, but the board needs to take concrete steps to demonstrate a commitment to securing diverse candidates. As the academic community across the country has raised concerns about a lack of diversity within university leadership, this must be a focus, from providing the committee with appropriate training to securing a search consultant who follows best practices in the recruitment process.[15] Given that the pool of traditional candidates is declining, removing the barriers for non-traditional candidates presents an opportunity to broaden the candidate pool and to increase the chances of finding an excellent candidate. The presidential recruitment process represents an opportunity for the board to demonstrate its commitment to equity, diversity, and inclusion.

The presidential search process is an important board process. The board does not often engage in such a high-profile way with the university community. The selection of the new president is one of the most important decisions the board will make. The process the board follows to make the selection is equally important for community-building and for laying the foundation for the new president to succeed.

C. SUPPORTING THE NEW PRESIDENT AFTER INSTALLATION

The installation of a new president at a university is exciting, and it comes with the pomp and ceremony appropriate to an institution that has an important place in society. Presidential colleagues, members of governments, and others with important connections to the university are invited to the installation ceremony. It is the official launch of the presidency. To support the president, the board should engage in a comprehensive training and initiation process, outlined below.

1) **Be clear about strategy.**[16] A good candidate brief and recruitment process will have set the stage for the conversation about strategy, because they should have outlined what the board believes are the strategic priorities. By the time the candidate is selected, there should already be good alignment on strategic priorities. This conversation should

---

15 Laura Godsoe & Jan Campbell, "Recruit Broadly: Advancing Diversity, Equity, and Inclusion," Knightsbridge Robertson Surrette (n.d.), online: KBRS www.kbrs.ca/insights/recruit-broadly-advancing-diversity-equity-and-inclusion.
16 Paul, above note 3 at 73; Stuart, above note 5 at 2.

continue, and should become more specific, so that there is clarity between the board and the president about expectations and the assessment of those expectations in the first year or two.

2) **Prepare the president for the university culture and the senior team.** Although the president will have engaged in due diligence during the course of the interview process, and should come to the university with a sense of the culture and some of the challenges, the board will be able to tell the new president more about the university, starting with the senior leadership team. With respect to the senior team, Katherine Haley suggests the following:

   i) "[A]ssess the senior team to understand its culture" and member dynamics and in particular identify those who will embrace change and those who might resist it.
   ii) Assess the "power bases and constituencies" of the senior team.
   iii) If any internal candidates have applied for the presidential role and have been unsuccessful, assess their "ability to take the high road—and to support the president who defeated them."
   iv) In many universities, the board must approve the hiring and termination of senior leaders on recommendation of the president. It will be helpful to the president to understand the board's willingness to make changes to the senior team.
   v) If possible, identify allies for the new president. These may include board members with tenure and experience on the board. One practice that may help is to create a president's transition advisory committee with trusted faculty, staff, and students from across the university.[17]

   It will be helpful for the board to identify other people of influence within the community who can advise and support the president. Particularly for those new to the presidential role, a mentor from another university may assist.

3) **Assess performance regularly.** The president's performance assessment should be an established part of the board's work. In the first year especially, reporting and feedback should be a regular occurrence. After the first year, objective setting and performance evaluation should be part of the annual board schedule. Discussions in which the president

---

17 Katherine Haley, "Team of Rivals" *Inside Higher Ed* (17 July 2019), online: www.insidehighered.com/advice/2019/07/17/why-and-how-boards-must-help-new-presidents-manage-their-senior-teams-opinion.

reports on accomplishments should be held during *in camera* sessions. The board should then have time to analyze and discuss this information in another *in camera* session, without the president.

4) **Prepare for and support a positive relationship between the board chair and the president.** Among board members, ideally the board chair has the closest relationship with the president. As Ross Paul notes, "A chair who understands the academic milieu and appreciates the challenges of dealing with so many interest groups from a relatively limited power base can do much to help a new president through difficult times."[18] At the same time, the president must be held accountable to the board.

5) **Foster trust between the board and the president and between both and the community.** There are many ways to foster trust. Acting with transparency is particularly important in the university context, and every university president and every board should demonstrate their commitment to transparency. One key way that the board can foster trust in both the board and the president, and also demonstrate accountability, is by conducting as much business as possible in public session. While university legislation generally allows for non-public meetings, the board should have a bias toward conducting as much business as possible in the public session, and the president should understand and support this.[19] Practices like these will build the president's credibility with the community.

It is important for the board to remember that its role is to support as well as manage the president. The board should have a plan for ensuring that the president feels supported.

---

18 Paul, above note 3 at 188.

19 Please note the distinction between non-public and *in camera*. University legislation or bylaws will typically give guidance as to what may be discussed in a non-public session of the board meeting. The board builds trust by having a bias toward public discussion, and justifying a non-public session by referring to the nature of the matter discussed. Non-public meetings should be restricted generally to human resources matters, other confidential matters such as litigation, or competitively sensitive information of third parties or the university. Non-public meetings should be minuted in confidential minutes. In contrast, *in camera* meetings are not minuted; no decisions should be made; and the sessions should be used as a time for the board to discuss a limited number of things, such as meeting management, materials, performance of staff, and in particular, feedback for the president.

D. CONCLUSION

While many question the effect a president can have on a large and unwieldy institution, selecting the right president is incredibly important. While the right candidate may not have as much of an effect as is hoped for by the board or the community, the wrong candidate can do a lot of damage to morale and reputation. It is crucial for the board to run a good, transparent, and inclusive search process. It is crucial for the board to canvas the university stakeholders for their views. The onboarding of the new president and a sustained focus on supporting the president while they navigate the unique challenges of this difficult role are also crucial. After reading this chapter, board members should understand the constraints within which a president operates and the challenges a president faces in leading these large institutions. In addition to managing the president's performance, the board must do all that it can to support the president and help them succeed.

CHAPTER 16

An Overview of University Finances

In Chapter 8, we began the discussion of the government's role in university finances. In this chapter, we take a closer look. This chapter is not about how to read balance sheets and university financial statements. When universities look for board members, they look for a certain number of members who have strong financial backgrounds and are financially literate, so that the board has the requisite expertise to oversee university finances. Even if you aren't recruited because of your financial expertise, you should learn to read financial statements. The focus of this chapter, however, is a further understanding of university finances and the issues the board and leadership team face in making financial decisions.

It won't surprise you to know that the financial picture for universities is complex. The board has a role in approving the budget and must understand the strategic choices and the risks associated with budget decisions. The board plays a primary role in ensuring the financial sustainability of the university. Board members should understand revenue sources, main categories of expenditures, and trends that underlie financial sustainability. This is not an easy thing to learn. There are provincial differences, and those will have an effect on your university. For example, in 2015, the Ontario government undertook a review of its post-secondary education funding formula and, in a bid to include other objectives,[1] switched from

---

1   Ben Lewis, "University Funding in Ontario and the Implications of the New Performance-Based Funding Model, a Discussion" *Academic Matters* (13 December 2017), online:

an enrolment-based funding model to a corridor model.² Glenn Craney, former Ontario Assistant Deputy Minister, Post-secondary Education Division, described the exercise as follows:

> Our north star for this was to shift away from a bums-in-seats model into something that starts to focus on other things . . . What the funding model does is it really starts to think through three major sections of how we support institutions. The first section is enrolment . . . we're not completely breaking the link that rewards enrolments. . . . We also wanted to have a portion of the model that starts to recognize other things . . . high quality student experiences, having quality programs, looking at research . . . looking at access . . . and then also thinking about what institutions need more broadly . . . [and] created a fund [that recognizes institutional impact on their community].³

The point here is that governments are looking at universities and trying to create incentives for behaviour or outcomes that advance government policy. As a board member, you should understand what governments are saying about changes in how money is spent.

A. FUNDING MODELS

Most provinces provide money to universities through a funding model. The model allocates the money to different universities within the province. Prince Edward Island and Newfoundland and Labrador have only one university each and no need for a model to help allocate funds.⁴ The other provinces allocate money based either on enrolment (e.g., Ontario and Saskatchewan), or on "a fixed share grant, which simply means that each institution's annual share is locked and moves up or down by the same percentage as the overall provincial quantum available for distribution" (e.g., British Columbia and Manitoba).⁵

---

      www.academicmatters.ca/university-funding-in-ontario-and-the-implications-of-the-new-performance-based-funding-model-a-discussion.

2 Higher Education Quality Council of Ontario, "The Ontario University Funding Model in Context" Government of Canada (June 2015), online: www.heqco.ca/SiteCollectionDocuments/Contextual%20Background%20to%20the%20Ontario%20University%20Funding%20Formula-English.pdf.

3 Lewis, above note 1.

4 *Ibid* at 8.

5 *Ibid*.

Both Ontario and Alberta have recently introduced performance-based funding models. Alberta's implementation was to have commenced 1 April 2020, and Ontario has implemented its model through Strategic Mandate Agreements completed in 2020. In Ontario's case, the funding model is based on ten metrics, and the goal was that within five years the majority of the operating fund transfer to universities would be based on meeting these performance targets.[6] Ontario has delayed implementation in the face of COVID-19 effects for the years 2020 through 2022.[7] Alberta has also indicated that it will delay implementation until 2021.[8] Under this model, the universities establish benchmarks against the metrics categories, and then report their progress against these benchmarks to the government. Board members should make it a point to understand the funding model that applies to the university. While the model should not dictate strategic direction, it should certainly inform strategic planning.

B. THE NATIONAL PICTURE: BACKGROUND INFORMATION FROM STATISTICS CANADA

The Organisation for Economic Cooperation and Development releases an annual study entitled "Education at a Glance," which is an assessment on the state of education around the world.[9] Among other things, the study looks at education participation rates and the amount of money spent on education. This study shows that there is a high rate of participation

---

6   Joe Friesen, "New Metrics for Ontario University and College Funding Include Employment and Graduation Rates" *Globe and Mail* (16 April 2019), online: www.theglobeandmail.com/canada/article-new-metrics-for-ontario-university-and-college-funding-include; Ryan White, "Province Unveils New Performance-Based Funding Structure for Post-Secondary Institutions" CTV News (20 January 2020), online: www.calgary.ctvnews.ca/province-unveils-new-performance-based-funding-structure-for-post-secondary-institutions-1.4775212.
7   Government of Ontario, News Release, "Promoting Excellence" Ontario Implements Performance Based Funding for Postsecondary Institutions" (26 November 2020), online: https://news.ontario.ca/en/release/59368/promoting-excellence-ontario-implements-performance-based-funding-for-postsecondary-institutions.
8   Demetrios Nicolaides, "Opinion: Post-Secondary Performance-Based Funding Delayed but Still Needed" *Edmonton Journal* (5 June 2020), online: https://edmontonjournal.com/opinion/columnists/opinion-post-secondary-performance-based-funding-delayed-but-still-needed.
9   Organisation for Economic Cooperation and Development, "Education at a Glance 2020" (Paris: OECD Publishing, 2020), online: www.oecd-ilibrary.org/education/education-at-a-glance-2020_69096873-en.

in higher education (colleges and universities) in Canada and that comparatively, "Canadian governments, collectively, fund higher education at a level higher that [sic] the OECD average."[10] To give you a sense of the financial magnitude of this sector, the 147 institutions in Canada permitted to grant degrees (noting that this includes colleges) collectively spent $28.9 billion in 2018/2019 (with no change from 2017/2018). Revenues increased by just over 3 percent to almost $31 billion.[11] Revenue losses associated with COVID-19 are expected in the range of $377 million to $3.4 billion.[12] These numbers are updated annually.

C. UNIVERSITY REVENUE

1) Government Funding

Here's what the latest Statistics Canada report ("Financial Information of Universities for the 2018/2019 School Year and Projected Impact of COVID-19 for 2020/2021") tells us about university revenue:

- Most revenue comes from government (45.8%) and tuition (29.4%).
- In 2018/2019, provincial funding rose slightly to $10.9 billion, as compared to $10.8 billion in 2017/2018.
- As a proportion of total funding, provincial funding has decreased over time, falling from 38.6% in 2013/2014 to 35.4% in 2018/2019.
- Federal government funding through research-granting programs was $3 billion in 2018/2019.
- Tuition brought in $9 billion in 2018/2019.
- "The share of revenues from tuition fees has grown (from 24.7% in 2013/2014 to 29.4% in 2018/2019).... An important element of this is the growing number of international students, who pay substantially higher tuition than domestic students and account for an increasing share of postsecondary students in Canada."
- Funds to support sponsored research come from the federal government, industry, and donors. Of the $3 billion in federal government

---

10 Alex Usher, "OECD Education at a Glance 2020," Higher Education Strategy Associates (9 September 2020), online: www.higheredstrategy.com/oecd-education-at-a-glance-2020.
11 Statistics Canada, "Financial Information of Universities for the 2018/2019 School Year and Projected Impact of COVID-19 for 2020/2021" (8 October 2020), online: www150.statcan.gc.ca/n1/daily-quotidien/201008/dq201008b-eng.htm at 1
12 Ibid at 1.

funding, "(93.4%) was directed toward sponsored research through research granting programs."

2) Tuition

Given the high degree of student and parent interest in tuition costs, it is worth understanding a little about tuition. In most institutions, the board is tasked with approving tuition. Tuition may be regulated (capped) by the provincial government. With respect to tuition, Statistics Canada also collects and shares great information:

- Average undergraduate tuition was $6,838 in 2018/2019 and average graduate tuition was $7,086.
- Dentistry, medicine, law, and pharmacy undergraduate programs (in that order) are the most costly programs.
- Tuition for other undergraduate programs in social and behavioural sciences ranged from $2,550 in Newfoundland and Labrador to $7,162 in Nova Scotia.
- Tuition in business, management, and public administration ranged from $2,792 (Quebec) to $10,570 (Ontario).
- The most costly graduate programs are MBAs.
- Mandatory ancillary fees such as fees for athletics, student health services and student associations" are increasing. Average undergraduate fees were $921 in 2018/2019.[13]

Boards should remember that tuition information does not tell the whole story of how much students are actually paying for their education. For example, 37 percent of students receive university scholarships, awards, or bursaries from the university to which they pay their tuition. These scholarships, awards, and bursaries are typically not financed from the operating budget, and instead come from donated funds or endowments.[14] Donors most often give money for a specific purpose by way of a donor agreement. Universities are then obligated to honour the commitment to use the funds for the purpose for which they are donated.

---

13 "Tuition Fees for Degree Programs, 2018/2019," Statistics Canada Catalogue no 11-001-X (5 September 2018), online: Statistics Canada www150.statcan.gc.ca/n1/en/daily-quotidien/180905/dq180905b-eng.pdf?st=pTRZ9zCu at 2 & 3.

14 Canadian University Survey Consortium, "2018 Graduating Student Survey Master Report," CUSC (June 2018), online: www.cusc-ccreu.ca/?page_id=32&lang=en at 36.

D. UNIVERSITY EXPENDITURES

Here's what we know about expenditures in the most recently reported years:

- Staff salaries, wages, and benefits make up the largest proportion of university expenditures at $16.7 billion in 2017/2018. Having said that, this number is a declining proportion of total expenditures, dropping from 59.3% in 2016/2017 to 57.7% in 2017/2018.
- Capital spending on items like real estate, equipment, and conducting large renovations comprised approximately 13% of total expenditures.[15]
- The remaining 30% is spent on the following:
    » goods and supplies — 9%
    » scholarships — 6%
    » services and fees — 5%
    » other — 10%[16]

E. FINANCIAL TRENDS

There are some trends of which boards should be aware:

- Government support for universities has been relatively flat for the last ten years.
- Tuition revenue has made up the revenue not provided by government, but it has been rising at the same rate as inflation, +1.5%.[17]
- Universities have increasingly relied on tuition from international students who pay much higher tuition than domestic students. In 2018/2019, "international students made up 15.7% of all university enrollments."[18]

---

15 "Financial Information of Universities and Degree-Granting Colleges, 2017/2018," above note 9 at 1.

16 Alex Usher, "Canadian University Expenses, 2017–18," Higher Education Strategy Associates (13 September 2019), online: www.higheredstrategy.com/canadian-university-expenses-2017-18.

17 Alex Usher, "Canadian University Finances 2017–18," Higher Education Strategy Associates (12 September 2019), online: www.higheredstrategy.com/canadian-university-finances-2017-18.

18 Alex Usher, "The State of Postsecondary Education in Canada, 2020" (Toronto: Higher Education Strategy Associates, 2020) at 19.

- "[F]or 6 of the last 8 years, Canadian universities as a whole have had a net surplus of less than one percent." As a point of reference, Australian and United Kingdom universities aim for surpluses in the 5% range.[19]
- While income is rising, expenditures are rising at the same rate "leaving them little room for manoeuvre should income ever fall."[20]
- The effects of COVID-19 will be to reduce university revenues anywhere from 6 to 12 percent in 2020 and for several years to come.[21]
- "[P]rofessional fees and external services, and scholarships" are "growing at above-average levels."[22]
- "Aggregate salaries for tenure-track academic salaries are growing slightly slower (7.9% over five years) than aggregate expenditures."[23]
- "[S]alaries for non-academics are growing slightly faster [than aggregate expenditures] at 10% over five years."[24]
- Allocating operating funds by function
  » academic faculties (instructional spending) — 59%
  » administration — 13%
  » student services — 10%
  » physical plant — 10%
  » technology — 4%
  » libraries — 4%[25]
- "[T]he biggest spending increases over the past 5 years are in student services ... followed by [information and communications technology]."[26]
- Overall university expenditures are increasing "pretty steadily at about inflation plus 2%."[27]
- Between 2005 and 2020, there has been a change in the programs students are taking. There has been significantly increased interest in science, technology, engineering, and mathematics (STEM) programs, and somewhat increased interest in health and business

---

19 Usher, 12 September 2019, above note 19.
20 *Ibid*.
21 Alex Usher, "Jobs," Higher Education Strategy Associates (21 May 2020), online: www.higheredstrategy.com/jobs.
22 Usher, 13 September 2019, above note 18.
23 *Ibid*.
24 *Ibid*.
25 *Ibid*.
26 *Ibid*.
27 *Ibid*.

programs. Interest in arts programs has decreased but stabilized. This has resulted in a realignment of the cost base for universities. It is much more expensive to teach subjects that involve labs and technology and equipment.[28] Alex Usher estimates that the shift in program interest alone has raised Ontario "per-student costs by 7%."[29] Usher notes that flat provincial funding means that the provinces did not fund this increased cost. Instead, Ontario universities funded the costs by charging higher tuition in "high demand fields: in Ontario, average tuition in engineering is about 85% higher than it is in the humanities, and business is about 50% more (on average . . .)."[30]

F. FINANCIAL ISSUES: WHAT CAUSES STAKEHOLDER CONCERNS?

There are many aspects of university finances that cause stakeholders to raise concerns. The following are issues that the board might hear about.

1) Budgeting Process

We've previously discussed the collegial and consultative nature of universities. Subject to your governing legislation, the board's general purview is the "business side" of the university, and the budget falls squarely into the business side of things. However, as noted in Chapter 12, your university legislation and bylaws may give a role in the budget process to the academic governing body, and this process should be respected and followed. Beyond that, however, there is a general expectation and likely a past practice of discussion of the budget with the academic governing body. As Ross Paul notes, the line of jurisdiction between academic planning and budget can never be absolute, and thus the board is well advised to ensure that stakeholder considerations inform their budget decisions. This does not mean that the board has to engage in these consultations. It does mean, however, that the board might ask how the budget decisions affect stakeholders.

---

28 Alex Usher, "The Shifting Cost-Base of Ontario's Higher Education System," Higher Education Strategy Associates (10 February 2020), online: www.higheredstrategy.com/the-shifting-cost-base-of-ontarios-higher-education.
29 Ibid.
30 Ibid.

It is particularly important in challenging fiscal times that the university community understand the budget process, and so the board should also be interested in how the budget process and the final budget are communicated to the university community. The board should explore how risk and risk management inform budget decisions. Another important concern is how budget decisions reflect university values and university strategy. The board and the senior leadership team will hear complaints from stakeholders who feel ill-informed, or who feel that the budget process was not transparent. To ensure the legitimacy of budget decisions, the board should concern itself with good process and communication.

2) Substantive Budget Concerns

Having come this far in the book, it will not surprise you to hear that stakeholders are very interested in substantive budget decisions, that is, how their universities spend money, and that there is a lot of disagreement about budget priorities. Students have concerns about tuition and student debt, and also about mandatory ancillary fees. Decisions relating to tuition and fees should be undertaken by the board with care and with an understanding of the interests and needs of the students. The board should understand financial aids available to students, as these may reduce the cost of tuition. Finally, the board should understand the regulatory and policy constraints within which it is operating. Peter MacKinnon objects to the amount of government control relating to tuition:

> Considering that government grant and tuition are the major fiscal instruments for operating a university, when governments control both, what role is there for a board to exercise its authority and take responsibility for its financial affairs?[31]

MacKinnon's point is well taken, and boards (and other stakeholders) are often frustrated by the many constraints they face in making budget decisions. MacKinnon goes on to note that the frustration of board members facing this high degree of government control undermines good governance. This is true. I note, however, that if boards give up in the face of this control, it will increase; and so boards must soldier on, managing all of the expectations and constraints as they do so.

---

31 Peter MacKinnon, *University Leadership and Public Policy in the Twenty-First Century: A President's Perspective* (Toronto: University of Toronto Press, 2014) at 39.

A key concern of faculty is the proportion of funds being spent on the core academic activities compared to that spent on administrative support and physical plant costs. The Canadian Association of University Teachers (CAUT) expresses concern about two things: (1) "a long-term trend [toward] a smaller share of total expenditures directed to faculty salaries," and (2) an increase in the use of contract academic staff who are paid less than full-time academic staff.[32] This concern was discussed in Chapter 6. Stakeholder concerns may or may not be valid. While CAUT suggests there is a consistent trend toward the increased use of contract staff, Alex Usher notes, for example, that "the percentage of total academic wages going to sessionals hit a 15-year low in 2017–18."[33]

Boards can expect the community to pay attention to both the budgeting process and to how budget decisions are reached. It is not the board's role to dive into the mechanics or the operational aspects of budgeting. However, the board should be sensitive to community concerns and should ensure that the budgeting process is compliant with the legislation (appropriate involvement from those who have a role in accordance with your legislation and bylaws), and further, that there is a good communication plan in place. It is not the board's role to evaluate individual budget decisions, but rather, to test the decision-making processes to ensure that the president and senior leadership team align budget decisions with university strategy and appropriate considerations of risk.

G. CONCLUSION

This chapter provides a high-level overview of university finances. Understanding revenue and expenditure sources and trends is important, as is understanding the role provincial and federal governments play in university finances. When considering financial matters, the board's focus is always on the bigger financial picture. This picture includes both risks (financial sustainability) and strategic direction. The board is asked to make financial decisions regularly — from approving material contracts or expenditures, to approving the annual financial statements. These financial decisions are important, but the board is not fulfilling its duty to the

---

32 Canadian Association of University Teachers, "Trends in University Finances in the New Millennium, 2000/01–2012/13," CAUT Education Review (2015), online: www.caut.ca/sites/default/files/caut-education-review-spring-2015.pdf at 11.

33 *Ibid.*

university if it doesn't also regularly consider the bigger picture and understand the implications of trends for your university.

The board's job is to ensure sustainability, and to do this it must understand the long-term financial picture, and those variables within the institution's control.

CHAPTER 17

Wrapping It Up: Some Important Conclusions

There's a lot more to write about university governance and I hope my colleagues continue to research and write about this important topic. I had to confine myself to certain topics, and I hope that what I chose to write about, and the amount of information I've provided, is helpful to those involved in university governance. In this final chapter, I'd like to emphasize some important messages.

Good governance is essential to university independence. Governance is important in any organization, but particularly in universities because universities are important on an individual and national level, they are the recipients of large amounts of public funds, and much is expected of them. As you join a university board, do so with pride, and don't lose sight of the broader mission of universities and the centrality of universities to the futures of many university stakeholders. Understand and strive to fulfil your fiduciary duty through a commitment to the interests of university stakeholders. Don't stop learning about your stakeholders, and never dismiss their interests.

The board's tone must be impeccable. Set a high standard of behaviour for the board, and make a clear and consistent commitment to transparency and integrity. Set the best example possible for the university community. The behaviour of some stakeholders (I'm thinking particularly of students and faculty) can be difficult to understand. It can make university leadership feel unappreciated, unheard, and can put it on the defensive. I've written before that there can be no "us versus them" mentality. All stakeholders are university stakeholders and all must be considered. Keep this in mind and help guide your leadership team.

The board must be brave and determined. Don't be daunted or intimidated by the academic environment, and whenever someone tells you "that's not how things are done in the university," don't take that at face value. Some things need to change, and long-standing practices aren't necessarily right. While some at universities would like to remain impenetrable and unaccountable, that is not what is expected of them. I wholeheartedly agree with those who see that if the current model of university governance fails, oversight will not be given to those inside universities. It is more likely that universities will be taken over by government or private commercial entities willing to play the accountability game and willing to be influenced, permeable, and adaptable. Universities are worthwhile protecting, and protecting them will mean walking the fine line between accountability and independence. Good governance is the balancing pole universities will need to walk this tightrope.

Academic governing bodies have a crucial role to play. Building links within the university will enable the board to build the appropriate links to government and the broader public—both necessary activities for university growth and sustainability. Fostering good governance practices within your university's academic governing body and supporting that body in its strategic initiatives is essential to building the links to stakeholders that universities need. Board members should understand the danger associated with faculty unions eclipsing the governing role of the university's academic governance body and should strenuously resist. Understanding key concepts like bicameralism and academic freedom will help.

Accountability and university autonomy are *not* mutually exclusive. Nothing good or sustainable happens quickly within universities, and boards who want to foster improvement and positive change must maintain a long-term focus and commitment to engaging their stakeholders in pursuit of the change they wish to bring about. Boards must help their internal stakeholders understand that autonomy and accountability are not mutually exclusive. Unless universities are able to fund themselves, they will be accountable. The extent to which accountability is permitted to diminish autonomy is determined by the board and senior management team. I believe this tension can be navigated such that all interests can be satisfied. To do this well, the board and senior leadership should clearly understand the goals of stakeholders to whom they are accountable, and at the same time should articulate their own goals of autonomy—what to protect and how to do it.

Passivity and good governance *are* mutually exclusive—hold management to account. Boards cannot be passive. Boards cannot accept reports at face value or be embarrassed to probe reports that are insufficient or that don't make sense to them. While it's important to support the president and the senior leadership team, and it's important to pick time and place and tone, it is crucial to ask probing and strategic questions. A good president understands that the board has a very important role to play. Fostering a culture of trust with the president and senior leadership will ensure that the board's anxiety about risks that are overlooked or strategies that are incomplete is received constructively in the spirit of working together in the best interests of the university. But even if board interventions are not welcome, they are sometimes necessary. Sometimes university leaders don't have their priorities straight. Sometimes university leaders resist necessary change. Sometimes university leaders fail to appropriately consider risks or stakeholder interests. Sometimes university leaders cannot see the shortcomings in university culture. It is essential to the effectiveness of university governance that the university see the board as independent and engaged. Engagement needs to be constructive, sensitive to the timing and tone of comment and criticism, and based on good intentions.

University governance professionals are crucial to good governance. Boards cannot underestimate the value of the support of effective governance professionals to ensuring good governance at your institution. When hiring governance professionals, ensure that they have the experience and background to support and guide the president and board in governance matters. Support the governance professionals as they support the board to navigate the jurisdictional, administrative, and political issues that boards will encounter. Appreciate how difficult the role can be and understand the skills required to do this well. The senior governance professional should have a formalized (solid or dotted line) relationship to the board chair. The governance professional is a crucial resource to the board as they navigates the complex university governance environment.

The buck stops with the board. All authority and accountability for the university ultimately rests with the board. Do not forget that you are a fiduciary charged with the highest obligations of trust to take care of the university. While matters are delegated to the president and that position's reports (and in some cases, to academic governing bodies), it is the board that is ultimately responsible for the financial sustainability and strategic direction of the university. Take this responsibility seriously. Engage. Learn. Question.

Closing with gratitude. Thank you for your commitment to university governance. Even if you've skimmed through this book, you will get a sense of how important effective governance is. Those who serve on university boards inevitably feel a sense of pride, as they should. Universities contribute to our societies on so many levels, and they could not do it without board members and those supporting them.

Bibliography

Academica Group Inc. "Canadian Institutions Issue Statements Against Racism." Article published 3 June 2020. www.academica.ca/top-ten/canadian-institutions-issue-statements-against-racism.

———. "Former Toronto Police Officer Says He Was Racially Profiled by McMaster Security." Article published 22 July 2020. www.academica.ca/top-ten/former-toronto-police-officer-says-he-was-racially-profiled-mcmaster-security.

———. "Student Group Urges UOttawa to End Carding on Campus." Article published 27 June 2019. www.academica.ca/top-ten/student-group-urges-uottawa-end-carding-campus.

———. "Today's Top Ten." Article published 15 October 2020. www.academica.ca/topten.

Acker, Sandra & Michelle Webber. "Discipline and Publish: The Tenure Review Process in Ontario Universities." In Lynette Shultz & Melody Viczko, *Assembling and Governing the Higher Education Institution*. London: Palgrave Macmillan, 2016.

Ali, Jennifer, Teresa Janz & Caryn Pearson. "Mental and Substance Use Disorders in Canada." Catalogue no 82-624-X Statistics Canada. September 2013. www.150.statcan.gc.ca/n1/en/pub/82-624-x/2013001/article/11855-eng.pdf?st=ckYHAplk.

Austin, Ian & Glen A Jones. *Governance of Higher Education: Global Perspectives, Theories and Practices.* New York: Routledge, 2016.

Bayern, Macy. "10 Technologies That Will Impact Higher Education the Most This Year." *Tech Republic*, Article published 29 March 2019 www.techrepublic.com/article/10-technologies-that-will-impact-higher-education-the-most-this-year.

Boggs, Andrew M. "Ontario's Royal Commission on the University of Toronto, 1905-06: Political and Historical Factors that Influenced the Final Report of the Flavelle Commission." MA thesis, University of Toronto, 2007. www.tspace.library.utoronto.ca/bitstream/1807/65526/1/Boggs_Andrew_M_2007_MA_thesis.pdf.

Birdsell Bauer, Louise & Karen Foster. "Out of the Shadows: Experiences of Contract Academic Staff." Canadian Association of University Teachers. Article published September 2018. www.caut.ca/sites/default/files/cas_report.pdf.

Bradshaw, James. "The Tricky Business of Funding a University." *Globe and Mail*, 17 October 2012, www.theglobeandmail.com/news/national/time-to-lead/the-tricky-business-of-funding-a-university/article4619883.

Broadbent Institute. "Disturbing Data from Statistics Canada Shows Anti-Indigenous Hate Crimes Are on the Rise." *PressProgress*. Article published 5 March 2020, www.pressprogress.ca/disturbing-data-from-statistics-canada-shows-anti-indigenous-hate-crimes-are-on-the-rise.

Burczycka, Marta. "Students' Experiences of Unwanted Sexualized Behaviours and Sexual Assault at Postsecondary Schools in the Canadian Provinces, 2019." Statistics Canada. 14 September 2020. wwww150.statcan.gc.ca/n1/pub/85-002-x/2020001/article/00005-eng.htm.

Business Insider. "Generation Z News: Latest Characteristics, Research, and Facts." n.d. www.businessinsider.com/generation-z.

Caboni, Timothy C. "Institutional Advancement in Higher Education: Historical Background, Areas of Institutional Advancement." Education Encyclopedia-State University. n.d. https://education.stateuniversity.com/pages/2088/Institutional-Advancement-in-Higher-Education.html.

Cambridge Dictionary. Cambridge University Press. n.d., www.dictionary.cambridge.org/dictionary/english/academe?q=Academe.

———. Cambridge University Press. n.d., www.dictionary.cambridge.org/dictionary/english/academia.

———. Cambridge University Press. n.d., www.dictionary.cambridge.org/dictionary/english/collegial.

Cameron, David M. *More Than an Academic Question: Universities, Government and Public Policy in Canada.* Halifax: The Institute for Research on Public Policy, 1991.

Canadian Alliance of Student Associations. "Members." n.d. www.casa-acae.com/members.

Canadian Association of University Business Officers. "About CAUBO." n.d., www.caubo.ca/discover-caubo/about-caubo.

Canadian Association of University Solicitors (CAUS). "Canadian Association of University Solicitors." n.d., https://caous.wildapricot.org.

Canadian Association of University Teachers. "About Us." n.d., www.caut.ca/about-us.

———. "Academic Freedom." Article published November 2018, www.caut.ca/about-us/caut-policy/lists/caut-policy-statements/policy-statement-on-academic-freedom.

———. "CAUT Policy Statement." Article published November 2019, www.caut.ca/about-us/caut-policy/ lists/caut-policy-statements/policy-statement-on-governance.

———. "Member Associations." n.d. www.caut.ca/about-us/members-locals.

———. "Ontario 'Free Speech' Requirements for Universities and Colleges Cause for Concern." Article published 31 August 2018. www.caut.ca/latest/2018/08/ontario-free-speech-requirements-universities-and-colleges-cause-concern.

———. "Shared Governance. Quality Education." n.d. www.caut.ca/campaigns/shared-governance.

———. "The Rise of Performance-Based Funding." Article published April 2020. www.caut.ca/ bulletin/2020/04/rise-performance-based-funding.

———. "Trends in University Finances in the New Millennium, 2000/01–2012/13." CAUT Education Review (2015). www.caut.ca/sites/default/files/caut-education-review-spring-2015.pdf.

Canadian Federation of Students (CFS). "Canadian Federation of Students." n.d., www.cfs-fcee.ca.

Canadian Universities Reciprocal Insurance Exchange (CURIE). "Failure to Educate ... Who is Failing Whom?" Published 2015, www.curie.org/sites/default/files/2016%20Educational%20Malpractice%20Bulletin%20-%20February%2011%202016%20(2).pdf.

Canadian University Boards Association. "CUBA 2020 AGM." n.d., www.cuba-accau.ca/Home.

Canadian University Survey Consortium. "2018 Graduating Student Survey Master Report." CUSC (June 2018). www.cusc-ccreu.ca/?page_id=32&lang=en.

CBC News. "Black UBC Graduate Student Alleges Racial Profiling on Campus." Article published 13 June 2020, www.cbc.ca/news/canada/british-columbia/black-ubc-graduate-student-alleges-racial-profiling-on-campus-1.5611316.

Council of Ontario Universities. "Council of Ontario Universities." n.d., www.cou.ca.

Davis, Brent. "Governance and Administration of Post Secondary Institutions in Canada." In Theresa Shanahan, Michelle Nilson & Li-Jeen Broshko, *Handbook of Canadian Higher Education Law*. Kingston: School of Policy Studies, Queen's University, 2015.

Davis, Darryn. "Two Queen's Graduate Students Speak Out About Their Experience with Racism in Kingston." *Global Kingston*, 2 October 2020. www.msn.com/en-ca/news/world/two-queens-graduate-students-speak-out-about-their-experience-with-racism-in-kingston/ar-BB18DazG?ocid=ientp.

Dwivedi, Supriya. "Rape Culture Persists in Our Legal System." *Toronto Sun*, 4 February 2016. www.torontosun.com/2016/02/04/rape-culture-persists-in-our-legal-system.

Dwyer, Mary. "Maclean's University Rankings 2020: Our Methodology." *Maclean's*, 3 October 2019. www.macleans.ca/education/macleans-university-rankings-2020-our-methodology.

———. "National Survey of Student Engagement: Results for Canadian Universities." *Maclean's*, 21 December 2018. www.macleans.ca/education/national-survey-of-student-engagement-results-for-canadian-universities/.

Eastman, Julia A et al. "Provincial Oversight and Institutional Autonomy: Findings of a Comparative Study of Canadian University Governance." 48 *Canadian Journal of Higher Education* 65 (2018).

Edelstein, Mark G. "Academic Governance: The Art of Herding Cats." In James Martin & James E Samels *First Among Equals: The Role of the Chief Academic Officer*. Baltimore: Johns Hopkins University Press, 1997.

Faucher, Kane X. "Welcome to a New Space for Adjunct Faculty." *University Affairs*, 5 February 2014). www.universityaffairs.ca/career-advice/contractually-bound/contractually-bound-welcome-to-a-new-space-for-adjunct-faculty.

Federation of Saskatchewan Indian Nations. *First Nations University of Canada Act, 2010*. www.fnuniv.ca/wp-content/uploads/2010_June_10_-_FN_University_of_Canada_Act_-_Amended.pdf.

Fidelman, Charlie. "Crisis on Campus: Universities Struggle with Students in Distress." *Montreal Gazette*, 27 May 2017. www.montrealgazette.com/news/local-news/mental-health-on-campus.

First Nations University of Canada. "Governance and Human Resources Committee Terms of Reference." Article published 29 July 2020. www.fnuniv.ca/governance.

Forgie, Sarah, Janice Miller-Young & Melina Sinclair. "Teaching Excellence and How It Is Awarded: A Canadian Case Study." 50 *Canadian Journal of Higher Education* 40 (2020).

Foy, Cheryl. "All Universities Should Have a General Counsel." *University Affairs*, 29 August 2019. www.universityaffairs.ca/?s=general+counsel.

———. "Reflections on the Tragedy of Flight 752." *University Affairs*, 17 January 2020. www.universityaffairs.ca/opinion/in-my-opinion/reflections-on-the-tragedy-of-flight-752.

Friesen, Joe. "New Metrics for Ontario University and College Funding Include Employment and Graduation Rates." *Globe and Mail*, 16 April 2019, www.theglobeandmail.com/canada/article-new-metrics-for-ontario-university-and-college-funding-include.

Giovannetti, Justin. "Doug Ford Says Ontario Postsecondary Schools Will Require Free-Speech Policies." *Globe and Mail*, 30 August 2018. www.theglobeandmail.com/canada/article-doug-ford-says-ontario-postsecondary-schools-will-require-free-speech.

Godsoe, Laura & Jan Campbell. "Recruit Broadly: Advancing Diversity, Equity, and Inclusion." Knightsbridge Robertson Surrette. n.d. KBRS www.kbrs.ca/insights/recruit-broadly-advancing-diversity-equity-and-inclusion.

Government of Canada. "Canada Student Loans and Grants." n.d., www.canada.ca/en/employment-social-development/programs/canada-student-loans-grants.html.

———. "Equity, Diversity and Inclusion Action Plan." Canada Research Chairs Program. Article published May 2017, www.chairs-chaires.gc.ca/program-programme/equity-equite/action_plan-plan_action-eng.aspx.

———. "Public Appointments." Article published 25 June 2018. www.ontario.ca/page/public-appointments.

———. "Terms of Reference." Royal Military College of Canada. n.d. www.rmc-cmr.ca/en/ college-commandants-office/terms-reference.

———. "The Ontario University Funding Model in Context." Higher Education Quality Council of Ontario. Published June 2015. www.heqco.ca/SiteCollectionDocuments/Contextual%20Background%20to%20the%20Ontario%20University%20Funding%20Formula-English.pdf.

Government of Ontario. "Broader Public Sector Accountability." Article published 26 August 2015. www.ontario.ca/page/broader-public-sector-accountability.

Government of Ontario. "Promoting Excellence: Ontario Implements Performance Based Funding for Postsecondary Institutions." News release, 26 November 2020. https://news.ontario.ca/en/release/59368/promoting-excellence-ontario-implements-performance-based-funding-for-postsecondary-institutions.

Graney, Emma. "'Blindsided': UCP Blasted for Mass Appointments to Boards, Commissions." *Edmonton Journal*, 17 August 2019. www.edmontonjournal.com/news/politics/ucp-mass-appoints-friends-to-20-public-boards-including-wcb-aglc-and-universities.

Grant, Tavia. "Hate Crimes in Canada Rose by 47 Per Cent Last Year: Statscan." *Globe and Mail,* 29 November 2018. www.theglobeandmail.com/canada/article-hate-crimes-in-canada-rose-by-47-per-cent-last-year-statscan.

Gravestock, Pamela & Emily Gregor Greenleaf. "Overview of Tenure and Promotion Policies Across Canada." University of Toronto. 2008. htttps://gov.viu.ca/sites/default/files/overviewoftppoliciesincanada.pdf.

Hakkareinen, Karen E. "A Smart Practice Guide to Presidential Transition: A Resource for Governing Boards and New Presidents of Canadian Public Universities." Master's project, University of Victoria, 2018. https://dspace.library.uvic.ca:8443/handle/1828/10561.

Haley, Katherine. "Team of Rivals." *Inside Higher Ed. Article published 17 July 2019.* www.insidehighered.com/advice/2019/07/17/why-and-how-boards-must-help-new-presidents-manage-their-senior-teams-opinion.

Henry, Francis et al. *The Equity Myth: Racialization and Indigeneity at Canadian Universities.* Vancouver: UBC Press, 2017.

Hicks, Martin & Linda Jonker. *Teaching Loads and Research Outputs of Ontario University Faculty Members: Implications for Productivity and Differentiation.* Toronto: Higher Education Quality Council of Ontario, 2014.

Indiana University Bloomington School of Education. "National Survey of Student Engagement Results." n.d. www.nsse.indiana.edu/index.html.

Jones, Glen A. "Trends in Academic Governance in Canada." University of Toronto. 28 January 2020. www.slideplayer.com/slide/6675800.

Keller, Lisa. "Enbridge Inquiry: University of Calgary President Was 'clearly' in conflict-of-interest." Canadian Association of University Teachers. Published 11 October 2017. www.caut.ca/latest/2017/10/enbridge-inquiry-university-calgary-president-was-clearly-conflict-interest.

Kuh, George D. "Four Ways Boards Can Help Students Succeed." Association of Governing Boards of Universities and Colleges. 2011. www.agb.org/trusteeship-article/four-ways-boards-can-help-students-succeed.

Lavender, Terry. "U of T Introduces New Teaching Stream Professorial Ranks." *U of T News*, 10 July 2015. www.utoronto.ca/news/u-t-introduces-new-teaching-stream-professorial-ranks.

Lewis, Ben. "University Funding in Ontario and the Implications of the New Performance-Based Funding Model, a Discussion." *Academic Matters*, 13 December 2017. www.academicmatters.ca/university-funding-in-ontario-and-the-implications-of-the-new-performance-based-funding-model-a-discussion.

MacDonald, Moira. "University Boards in the Spotlight." *University Affairs*, 3 January 2018. www.universityaffairs.ca/features/feature-article/university-boards-spotlight.

MacKinnon, Peter. *University Commons Divided: Exploring Debate & Dissent on Campus*. Toronto: University of Toronto Press, 2018.

———. *University Leadership and Public Policy in the Twenty-First Century: A President's Perspective*. Toronto: University of Toronto Press, 2014.

Maclean's. "University Rankings 2020." Article published 3 October 2019. www.macleans.ca/education/university-rankings/university-rankings-2020.

Martin, James & James E Samels. *First Among Equals: The Role of the Chief Academic Officer*. Baltimore: Johns Hopkins University Press, 1997.

Martis, Eternity. *They Said This Would Be Fun: Race, Campus Life, and Growing Up*. Toronto: Penguin Random House, 2020.

Massey, Jennifer, Sean Field & Yolande Chan. "Partnering for Economic Development: How Town-Gown Relations Impact Local Economic Development in Small and Medium Cities." 44 *Canadian Journal of Higher Education* 152 (2014).

Murphy, Steven. "Tech with a Social Conscience: Why You Should Care." *Globe and Mail*, 17 April 2019. www.theglobeandmail.com/business/careers/leadership/article-tech-with-a-social-conscience-why-you-should-care.

National Survey of Student Engagement. *Engagement Insights: Survey Findings on the Quality of Undergraduate Education — Annual Results 2017*, Bloomington: Indiana University Center for Postsecondary Research, 2017.

Nicolaides, Demetrios. "Opinion: Post-Secondary Performance-Based Funding Delayed but Still Needed." *Edmonton Journal*, 5 June 2020. https://edmontonjournal.com/opinion/columnists/opinion-post-secondary-performance-based-funding-delayed-but-still-needed.

Organisation for Economic Cooperation and Development. "Education at a Glance 2020." Paris: OECD Publishing, 2020. www.oecd-ilibrary.org/education/education-at-a-glance-2020_69096873-en.

Oshawa Express. "Northern Dancer: Little Horse, Big Legacy." Article published 18 April 2018. www.oshawaexpress.ca/northern-dancer-little-horse-big-legacy.

Pasma, Chandra & Erika Shaker. *Contract U: Contract Faculty Appointments at Canadian Universities.* Ottawa: Canadian Centre for Policy Alternatives, 2018.

Paul, Ross. *Leadership Under Fire: The Challenging Role of the Canadian University President.* Montreal: McGill-Queen's University Press, 2011.

Pennock, Lea et al. "Academic Senates and University Governance in Canada: Changes in Structure and Perceptions of Senate Members." Paper delivered at the annual meeting of the Consortium of Higher Education Researchers, Belgrade, Serbia, 10–12 September 2012.

———. "Challenges and Opportunities for Collegial Governance at Canadian Universities: Reflections on a Survey of Academic Senates." 46 *Canadian Journal of Higher Education* 73 (2016).

Piereson, James & Naomi S Riley. "Donors Beware: Universities and Museums Find It Harder and Harder to Accept Financial Gifts That Don't Set Off Political Controversy." *City Journal*, 19 November 2019. www.city-journal.org/donors-political-controversy.

Quacquarelli Symonds. "QS World University Rankings." n.d. www.qs.com.

Queen's University. *Consolidated Royal Charter, 2001.* www.queensu.ca/secretariat/sites/webpublish.queensu.ca.uslcwww/files/files/index/RoyalCharter2011.pdf.

———. *Queen's Encyclopedia.* n.d., www.queensu.ca/encyclopedia/c/chancellors.

Ricci, Sandrine & Manon Bergeron. "Tackling Rape Culture in Québec Universities: A Network of Feminist Resistance." 25 *Violence Against Women* 1290 (2019).

Shanahan, Theresa, Michelle Nilson & Li-Jeen Broshko. *Handbook of Canadian Higher Education Law*. Kingston: School of Policy Studies, Queen's University, 2015.

ShanghaiRanking Consultancy. "Academic Ranking of World Universities." n.d. www.shanghairanking.com.

Shen, Anqi. "Universities Take Steps to Tackle Food Insecurity on Campus." *University Affairs*, 7 March 2019. www.universityaffairs.ca/news/news-article/universities-take-steps-to-tackle-food-insecurity-on-campus.

Silverthorn, Drew. *Hungry for Knowledge: Assessing the Prevalence of Student Food Insecurity on Five Canadian Campuses*. Toronto: Meal Exchange, 2016.

Statistics Canada. "Financial Information of Universities and Degree-Granting Colleges, 2017/2018." Statistics Canada Catalogue no 11-001-X. Published 24 July 2019. www150.statcan.gc.ca/n1/daily-quotidien/190724/dq190724a-eng.pdf.

———. "Full-Time Teaching Staff at Canadian Universities, 2017/2018." Published 14 December 2018. www150.statcan.gc.ca/n1/pub/11-627-m/11-627-m2018056-eng.htm.

———. "Leading Causes of Death, Total Population, by Age Group." Statistics Canada Table: 13-10-0394-01. Published 2016. www150.statcan.gc.ca/t1/tbl1/en/tv.action?pid=1310039401.

———. "Number of Full-time Teaching Staff at Canadian Universities, by Rank, Sex." Statistics Canada Table: 37-10-0076-01. Published 2019. www150.statcan.gc.ca/t1/tbl1/en/tv.action?pid=3710007601.

———. "Survey of Postsecondary Faculty and Researchers, 2019." Published 22 October 2020. www150.statcan. gc.ca/n1/daily-quotidien/200922/dq200922a-eng.htm.

———. "Tuition Fees for Degree Programs, 2018/2019." Statistics Canada Catalogue no 11-001-X. Published 5 September 2018. www150.statcan.gc.ca/n1/en/daily-quotidien/180905/dq180905b-eng.pdf?st=pTRZ9zCu.

———. "UCASS Revisited." Article published 18 January 2018. www.statcan.gc.ca/eng/blog/cs/ucass-revisited.

———. "Union Status by Industry." Statistics Canada Table: 14-10-0132-01. Published 2019. www150.statcan.gc.ca/t1/tbl1/en/tv.action?pid=1410013201.

Stuart, Anna. "The Case for Change: Reimagining the Academic Leadership Search Process." Knightsbridge Robertson Surrette. n.d. www.kbrs.ca/insights/case-change-reimagining-academic-leadership-search-process.

———. "What is Leadership." Knightsbridge Robertson Surrette. February 2013. www.kbrs.ca/sites/default/files/viewpoint_feb.pdf.

Stuart, Anna, Ross Paul & Peter George. "Leadership in Academia: Onboarding." Knightsbridge Robertson Surrette. 2012. www.kbrs.ca/insights/leadership-academia-onboarding.

Times Higher Education. "THE World University Rankings." n.d. www.timeshighereducation.com/world-university-rankings/2021/world-ranking#!/page/0/length/25/sort_by/rank/sort_order/asc/cols/stats.

U Sports. "U Sports." n.d. https://usports.ca/en.

U15 Group of Canadian Research Universities. "Group of Canadian Research Universities." n.d. www.u15.ca.

Universities Canada. "About Us." n.d., www.univcan.ca/about-us.

———. "Advancing Reconciliation Through Higher Education: 2017 Survey Findings." Article published April 2018. www.univcan.ca/wp-content/uploads/2018/10/Indigenous_survey_findings_2017_factsheet_25Apr_.pdf.

———. "Facts and Stats." Article published 31 July 2018. www.univcan.ca/universities/facts-and-stats/.

———. "Member Universities." n.d. www.univcan.ca/universities/member-universities.

———. "Priorities." n.d. www.univcan.ca/priorities.

———. "Provincial Quality Assurance Systems." n.d. www.univcan.ca/universities/quality-assurance/provincial-quality-assurance-systems.

———. "Statement on Academic Freedom." Article published 25 October 2011. www.univcan.ca/media-room/media-releases/statement-on-academic-freedom.

———. "Universities Canada Principles on Equity, Diversity, and Inclusion." Article published 26 October 2017. www.univcan.ca/media-room/media-releases/universities-canada-principles-equity-diversity-inclusion.

———. "Universities Canada Principles on Indigenous Education." Article published 29 June 2015. www.univcan.ca/media-room/media-releases/universities-canada-principles-on-indigenous-education.

University of Ontario Institute of Technology and The University of Ontario Institute of Technology Faculty Association. "Collective Agreement Between The University of Ontario Institute of Technology and The University of Ontario Institute of Technology Faculty Association." Published 4 March 2019. www.shared.uoit.ca/shared/department/hr/Working-at-UOIT/faculty-association---collective-agreement,-effective-march-4,-2019-to-june-30,-2021.pdf.

University of Saskatchewan. "Governance Office." n.d. https://governance.usask.ca.

University of Toronto. "Canadian Universities and Colleges Come Together to Take Action on Anti-Black Racism." *U of T News*. Article published 16 July 2020. www.utoronto.ca/news/u-t-led-national-dialogue-address-anti-black-racism-higher-education.

Usher, Alex. "2020 Rankings Round-Up." Higher Education Strategy Associates. Published 8 September 2020. www.higheredstrategy.com/2020-rankings-round-up.

———. "Canadian University Expenses, 2017–18." Higher Education Strategy Associates. Published 13 September 2019. www.higheredstrategy.com/canadian-university-expenses-2017-18.

———. "Canadian University Finances 2017–18." Higher Education Strategy Associates. Published 12 September 2019. www.higheredstrategy.com/canadian-university-finances-2017-18.

———. "Jobs." Higher Education Strategy Associates. Published 21 May 2020. www.higheredstrategy.com/jobs.

———. "OECD Education at a Glance 2020." Higher Education Strategy Associates. Published 9 September 2020. www.higheredstrategy.com/oecd-education-at-a-glance-2020.

———. "The Shifting Cost-Base of Ontario's Higher Education System." Higher Education Strategy Associates. Published 10 February 2020. www.higheredstrategy.com/the-shifting-cost-base-of-ontarios-higher-education.

———. "The State of Postsecondary Education in Canada, 2020." Toronto: Higher Education Strategy Associates, n.d.

Walton, Gerald. "Academic Underperformers Must Be Called Out." *University Affairs*, 9 January 2017. www.universityaffairs.ca/opinion/in-my-opinion/academic-underperformers-must-called.

Weingarten, Harvey P., Linda Jonker, Amy Kaufman & Martin Hicks. "University Sustainability: Expenditures." Toronto: Higher Education Quality Council of Ontario, 2018. https://heqco.ca/pub/university-sustainability-expenditures.

White, Ryan. "Province Unveils New Performance-Based Funding Structure for Post-Secondary Institutions." CTV News. 20 January 2020. www.calgary.ctvnews.ca/province-unveils-new-performance-based-funding-structure-for-post-secondary-institutions-1.4775212.

Wicks, Victoria. "Does U of T Student Life Condone Rape Culture?" *The Varsity*, 31 March 2014. www.thevarsity.ca/2014/03/31/does-u-of-t-student-life-condone-rape-culture.

Wikimedia Foundation Inc. *Wikipedia*. n.d. https://en.wikipedia.org/wiki/Academy.

Young, David & Wendy Kraglund-Gauthier. "Governance and Administration of Postsecondary Education Associations: A Vital Piece of the Postsecondary Governance Structure." In Theresa Shanahan, Michelle Nilson & Li-Jeen Broshko, *Handbook of Canadian Higher Education Law*. Kingston: School of Policy Studies, Queen's University, 2015.

Zoledziowski, Anya. "Lack of Faculty Diversity Can Affect Studies and Career Aspirations." *Globe and Mail*, 18 October 2017. www.theglobeandmail.com/news/national/education/canadian-university-report/lack-of-faculty-diversity-can-affect-studies-and-career-aspirations/article36637410.

Index

T after a page number indicates a table.

Academic freedom
  about, 99, 101
  fiduciary duty, vs, 105–6
  freedom of expression (speech), vs, 103–4
  importance, 99
  limits, 105–6
  protection of, 98–99, 100, 102, 105–6
  responsibilities, 99–101
  rights, 101–2
  statement (Universities Canada), 99–101
Academic governing body (senate)
  board relationship, 2, 111, 121–22, 125, 159–67, 171
  collegial management, 2, 171
  composition of, 118T–19T
  democratic management, 171
  effectiveness vs ineffectiveness, 119, 121–22, 161–67
  institutional differences, 160
  names of, 124–25
  non-academic members, 162–63
  powers, 125–26, 146T–58T, 166
  president as chair, 61
  purview, 125
  role, 119, 160, 191
  shared governance, 159–61
  unionization effects, 162, 164–66
Academic Ranking of World Universities, 89
Academic words (definitions), 90–91
Academica Group (Top Ten), 71
Access Copyright, 87, 87n17
Adell-Carter study, 164
Administration. *See also* Presidents
  academic administrators, 59
  advancement executive, 63–64
  associations, 83–84
  chancellor, 60–61
  chief academic vs chief executive officer, 61–62
  chief financial officer, 63, 65
  chief research officer, 62–63
  functions, 59, 65
  governance professionals, 16–17, 64, 167–68, 192
  internal stakeholder, 59–65
  legal counsel, 64–65
  organizational structure, 60
  provost, 61
  roles, 60–65
  university secretary, 16–17, 64

Alberta
    board recruitment practices, 70
    freedom of speech cases, 103
    performance-based funding, 70, 181
    tenure, 55T
    university legislation, 55, 68T, 70, 109
Algoma University (ON), 76, 113T–14T, 114n5
Allingham, Douglas, 9
Anti-Black racism, 29–30, 40
Association of Governing Boards of Colleges and Universities (AGB), 123n2
Associations. See Groups and associations
Austin, Ian, 52, 94
Autonomy. See Institutional autonomy

Bayern, Macy, 32–33
BCE v 1976 Debentureholders case, 13–14, 15
Berdahl, Professor Jennifer (UBC), 104–5
Best practice tips
    board authority, 124
    board decisions, 15
    board governance, 121–22, 124
    conflict of interest, 20
Bicameral governance, 96–98, 163
Bishop's University (QC) statutes
    academic governing body powers, 146T–58T
    governing board powers, 123, 127T–45T
    shared governance, 160
Black Lives Matter, 35, 40
Black racism, 29–30, 40
Board governance. See University board governance
Board of Trustees Conflict of Interest Policy (Brock University), 23
British Columbia *University Act*
    about, 68T, 109, 110, 110n4
    academic governing body powers, 146T–58T
    board powers, 55T, 123, 127T–45T
    government powers, 68T
    shared governance, 160
    tenure, 55T
Brock University (ON), 23
Brown University (US), 78

Cameron, David, 66–67, 69, 162, 164
Canada (education participation rates and funding), 182
Canada Education Savings Act (2004), 73
Canada Health and Social Transfer (CHST), 72
Canada Research Chairs Program (CRCP), 50
Canada Student Loans Program, 73
Canadian Alliance of Student Associations (CASA), 88
Canadian Association of University Business Officers (CAUBO), 83
Canadian Association of University Solicitors (CAUS), 83
Canadian Association of University Teachers (CAUT). *See also* Faculty
    about, 83, 86–87, 87n17
    academic freedom, 87, 101–2, 105
    contract vs full-time academic staff, 57, 188
    donor interference, 77
    faculty governance role, 97–98, 162, 163
    free-speech policies, 93
    policy statement, 101–2
    unionization, 164–65
Canadian Charter of Rights and Freedoms (1982), 103
Canadian Federation of Students (CFS), 88
Canadian Interuniversity Sport (CIS/U Sports), 84–85
Canadian Universities Reciprocal Insurance Exchange (CURIE), 43
Canadian University Boards Association (CUBA), 83–84
Carleton University (ON)
    academic freedom, 77, 105–6, 115–16
    donor interference, 77
    faculty association, 105–6
    freedom of expression (speech) vs academic freedom, 105–6
Collegiality (definition), 94
Community, 75–81
    creative economy, 79
    donors, 76–78
    Indigenous peoples, 75–76, 81

moral stakeholder, as, 80
present vs future, 80
university (town-gown relations), 79–80
Confidentiality, 14
Conflict of interest
  about, 18–20
  avoidance obligation, 14, 19, 115–16
  being in, 19
  declaration of, 20–22
  example of, 21–22
  financial, 20
  identification of, 20
  internal members, 115–16
  objectivity, and, 19
  personal, 20, 22–23
  removal from, 19
Constitution Act (1867), 66
Council of Ontario Universities, 83
COVID-19 (coronavirus) pandemic
  funding delays, 181
  revenue losses, 182, 185
  student waivers, 44
Craney, Glenn, 180
Creative economy, 79
Crenshaw, Kimberlé, 30

Diligence, 16, 27–33
Diversity and inclusion. *See* Equity, diversity, and inclusion
Donors, 76–78, 183
Duff-Berdahl Commission, 163, 166

Eastman, Julia, 92–93
Education participation rates, 181–82
Enbridge, 77
Equity, diversity, and inclusion
  cultural change, 28
  faculty and student survey, 50–51
  intersectionality, 30
  presidents (candidates), 175
  principles, 29–30
  students, 36–37
External stakeholders, 66–89
  about, 66
  community, 75–81
  government, 66–74
  groups and associations, 82–89

Faculty, 46–58. *See also* Canadian Association of University Teachers (CAUT); Universities
  academic freedom, 100–2, 104–6
  academic governing bodies, 118T
  academic quality, 58
  academic ranks, 47T, 53
  age demographics, 49, 51–52
  autonomy vs donor interference, 77–78
  clinical, 47
  collective agreements, 56–57
  contract vs tenured, 57–58, 188
  freedom of expression (speech), 93, 104–5
  full-time categories, 46–47T
  industry partnerships, 78
  numbers, 46–47T
  part-time contracts, 57–58
  political interference, 92, 92n6
  productivity statistics, 48
  professor rank, 47T, 53
  racial composition, 49–51
  retirement, 51–52
  roles and responsibilities, 100–1
  self-government, 162–63
  surveys, 162–63
  tenure appointments, 53–55T, 56–57
  unionization, 52, 96–98
  visible minorities, 49–51
  women, 49–51
  work areas, 48–49
Federal government
  funding, 62, 72–73, 182–83
  provincial government relationship, vs, 66–67
  registered education savings programs, 73
  research and innovation funding, 50, 62, 72–73
  role, 72–73
  student grants and loans, 73
  transfer payments, 72
Fiduciary duty, 13–17
  about, 13–14
  academic freedom, vs, 103, 105–6
  academic governing body, 97
  behavioural obligations, 14–15

business judgment rule, 15
duty of care, 15–16
governance professional, 16–17
hat metaphor, 17
Finances. *See* University finances
Financial conflict of interest, 20
First Nations University of Canada (Saskatchewan Indian Federated College), 75
Flavelle Commission (1906), 92, 92n6, 96
Floyd, George, 29
Freedom of expression (speech), 103–5

Germany, 115
Gorelick, Professor Root (Carleton), 105–6, 115–16
Governance. *See* University board governance
Governance professionals, 16–17, 64, 167–68, 192
Government, 66–74. *See also* Federal government; Provincial government
  about, 66, 74
  education participation rates and funding, 182
  funding models, 179–81
  municipal, 73
  tuition control, 121, 187
Groups and associations, 82–89. *See also* specific names of associations
  academic, 82–83
  administrative, 83–84
  faculty, 83, 93, 96–98, 105–6, 162, 163
  national, 85–87n19, 88
  role, 89
  types, 82–85
Gupta, Arvind (UBC President), 104–5

Haley, Katherine, 176
Handbook of Canadian Higher Education Law, 67, 72
Hashmani, Karima, 29n1
Higher Education Quality Council of Ontario (HEQCO), 48

Inclusion. *See* Equity, diversity, and inclusion

Indigenous peoples
  faculty, 50–51
  racism (students), 41
  stakeholders, 75–76
  Truth and Reconciliation Commission (TRC) report, 41, 76, 81
Institutional autonomy. *See also* Universities
  academic freedom, 100
  academic governing body (senate), 166
  bicameral governance, and, 96, 96n21
  board accountability, 191–92
  donor interference, vs, 77–78
  good governance, 2, 120–22, 190–92
  government control, vs, 91–92, 92n6, 93–94
Internal stakeholders
  administration, 59–65
  faculty, 46–58
  students, 34–45
Intersectionality, 30

Jones, Glen, 52, 94, 165–66

Lakehead University (ON), 113T–14T
Lieutenant Governor in Council appointments (LGICs Ontario), 70–71, 92n6

MacKinnon, Peter
  bicameral governance, 96, 96n21, 97–98
  conflict of interest, 115–16
  constituency factor, 116
  faculty unionization, 165
  fiduciary duty vs academic freedom, 105–6
  good governance, 120–21
  president, 171
  self-governance, 120–21
  students, 35
  tuition control, 187
  universities as commons, 91
  university complexity, 9
Maclean's rankings, 88, 88n22
Manitoba
  board recruitment practices, 71
  performance-based funding, 70
  university legislation, 68T

Martis, Eternity, 40
Massey, Jennifer, 79
McGill University (QC)
   alumni relations, 44–45
   board composition, 113T–14T
McMahon, Justice, 77
Memorial University of Newfoundland (NL), 113T–14T
Montalbano, John, 104–5
Mount Allison University (NB) *Act*
   academic governing body powers, 146T–58T
   governing board powers, 123, 127T–45T
Municipal government, 73
Murphy, Dr Steven, 32

National Survey of Student Engagement (NSSE/"Nessie"), 36, 88
New Brunswick
   performance-based funding, 70
   university legislation, 68T
Newfoundland and Labrador
   government funding models, 180
   university legislation, 68T
Northern Dancer (racehorse), 80
Nova Scotia College of Art and Design, 45
Nova Scotia university legislation, 68T

Ontario
   board recruitment practices, 70–71
   executive compensation legislation, 174
   fixed share grant funding, 180
   free-speech policies, 93
   government funding model, 179–80
   government vs institutional autonomy, 91–92, 92n6, 93
   performance-based funding, 69, 181
   regional relevance (universities), 79, 79n9
   research universities, 83
   tuition rates, 186
   university legislation, 68T
Ontario Public Appointments Secretariat, 70–71
Ontario Tech University. *See* University of Ontario Institute of Technology (ON)

Organisation for Economic Cooperation and Development (OECD) education study, 181–82

Paul, Ross, 161, 170, 172, 186
Pennock, Lea, 118, 119, 165, 167
Personal conflict of interest, 20
Post-Secondary Learning Act (Alberta), 68T, 70
Presidents. *See also* University board governance
   academic freedom, 100
   advisors, 176
   appointment failures, 169n1
   board chair relationship, 177
   board relationship, 169–78
   candidates (equity, diversity, and inclusion), 175
   challenges, 170–72
   community engagement, 174
   compensation, 174
   leadership competencies, 100, 170–71
   performance assessment, 176–77
   priorities, 175–76
   recruitment process and search committee, 172–75
   role, 61, 100, 167, 170–72
   training and initiation, 175–77
   transparency, 177
   trust and credibility, 177
   university culture knowledge, 172, 176
Prince Edward Island
   government funding models, 180
   university legislation, 68T
Provincial government
   board appointees, 70–71
   degree granting authority, 69
   educational authority, 66, 67–68T, 69, 70–71, 74
   federal government relationship, vs, 66–67
   fixed share grant funding, 180
   funding models, 69–70, 179–82
   institutional autonomy, vs, 91–94
   performance-based funding, 69–70, 181
   university legislation, 67–68T, 69, 74

QS World University Rankings, 88
Quebec
  student associations, 88
  university legislation, 68T
Quebec Student Union, 88
Queen's University (ON)
  alumni relations, 44
  chancellor, 60–61
  charter, 55T, 110
  racism, 40

Racism
  anti-Black, 29–30, 40
  diversity and inclusion initiatives, 27–28, 29–30
  Indigenous, 41
Rape culture, 39
Robinson, David, 97–98
Ross, Murray, 95n19
Rowat survey, 162–63
Royal Military College (RMC), 110

Saskatchewan
  fixed share grant funding, 180
  performance-based funding, 70
  university legislation, 68T
Saskatchewan Indian Federated College (First Nations University of Canada), 75
Senate. See Academic governing body (senate)
Sexual violence statistics, 38–39
Shanahan, Theresa, 72
Shared governance, 159–68
Social issues (students), 37–41
  disabilities and accommodation for, 38
  mental health, 37–38
  priorities, 37–41
  racism, 40–41
  sexual violence, 38–39
  suicide statistics, 38
St. Francis Xavier University (NS)
  alumni relations, 44
  board composition, 113T–14T
Stakeholders. See also Administration; Community; Faculty; Government; Groups and associations; Students

board accountability, 191–92
board appointees, 117
board as stakeholder board, 18
board diligence, 27–28
  external, 66–89
  financial concerns, 186–88
  internal, 34–65
  multi, 28–33
Statistics Canada report, 182–83
Students, 34–45. See also Universities
  alumni, 44–45
  associations, 84–85, 88
  athletics, 84–85
  debt, 41–42
  demographics, 34–35, 36–37
  disabilities and accommodation for, 38
  educational malpractice (failure to educate) claims, 42–44
  engagement level, 35–36
  equity, diversity, and inclusion, 36–37
  fees, 84
  financial aids, 187
  grants and loans, 73
  Indigenous, 41
  international, 34, 36, 184
  mental health, 37–38
  numbers, 34
  registered education savings programs, 73
  sexual violence, 38–39
  social issues, 37–41
  suicide statistics, 38
  technology, 31–33
  tuition, 41–42, 183, 186
Suicide statistics (students), 38
Supreme Court of Canada (SCC), 14, 15

Technology, 31–33
TED talks, 30
Tettey, Dr Wisdom, 29n1
THE World University Rankings, 88
Thompson Rivers University Act (2005), 110n4
Top Ten (Academica Group), 71
Tricameral governance, 96
Truth and Reconciliation Commission of Canada (TRC) report, 41, 76, 81

Index

U Sports (Canadian Interuniversity Sport (CIS)), 84–85
U15 group (research universities), 82–83
Unicameral governance, 95, 95n19
Unionization
   bicameral governance, 96–98
   collective agreements, 56–57
   effects on academic governing bodies, 162, 164–66
   rates, 52
   tenure, 56–57
United States, 78, 79, 123n2
Universities. *See also* Faculty; Institutional autonomy; Students; University culture and concepts; University finances
   alumni relations, 44–45
   Charter case, 103
   competition, 42
   complex organization, as, 8–9
   creative economy, 79
   cultural change, 28–29
   culture and concepts, 90–106
   donors, 76–78
   educational malpractice (failure to educate) claims, 42–44
   equity, diversity and inclusion, 28–30
   finance administration and operations, 63, 65
   freedom of expression (speech), 104–6
   free-speech policies, 93
   fundraising, 63–64, 76–77
   human resources, 60
   indigenization, 76
   industry partnerships, 78
   insurance coverage, 43
   labour relations, 52, 56–57
   legal counsel, 83, 103
   legislation and bylaws, 54–55T, 67–68T, 109–11, 123–24, 127T–58T
   litigation, 42–44, 87n17
   local community (town-gown relations), 79–80
   municipal government role, 73
   national associations, 85–87n19, 88
   numbers of, 1, 1n2
   organizational structure, 60
   performance-based funding, 69–70, 181
   policies, 111–12
   provincial authority, and, 66, 67–68T, 69, 70–71, 74
   racism, 27–28, 29–30, 40–41
   rankings entities, 88–89
   rape culture, 39
   research and innovation, 50, 62–63, 72–73, 82–83
   societal role, 8
   technological implications on, 32–33
Universities Canada ((UC) Association of Universities and Colleges of Canada)
   about, 82, 85–86
   academic freedom statement, 99–101
   bicameral governance and membership criteria, 95
   freedom of expression (speech) vs academic freedom, 104
   member universities, 67
University autonomy. *See* Institutional autonomy
University board governance. *See also* Presidents; University governance structure
   about, 1
   academic governing body relationship, 2, 111, 121–22, 125, 159–67, 171
   accountability, 191–92, 193
   annual policy reports, 112
   best practices tips, 15, 20, 121–22, 124
   bicameral, 95–98, 163
   board chair, 177
   board composition, 112–14T
   budget process and decisions, 125, 186–88
   challenges, 8–9
   collegial management, 171
   committee authority, 124
   decision-making and business judgment rule, 15
   democratic management, 171, 173
   engagement and intervention, 192
   financial trends awareness, 184–86, 188–89
   forms of, 95–96
   functions of, 122–23

good governance, 2, 120–22, 190–93
governance professional role, 64, 192
governing body names, 127T
government relations, 74
institutional differences, 160
legal counsel, 64–65
legislative powers, 127T–45T
membership considerations, 7–12
policy framework, 111–12
powers, 123–24, 127T–45T
president recruitment, 172–75
president relationship with, 169–78
reforms, 163
role, 120–22
shared, 159–68
stakeholder board, as, 18
standards, 190–91
transparency, 177
tricameral, 96
unicameral, 95, 95n19
university secretary role, 16–17, 64
University board meetings
  in camera vs non-public sessions, 177, 177n19
  conflict of interest discussions, 19–20, 21–22
  decisions and business judgment rule, 15
  minutes, 10
  orientation sessions, 124
University board members
  associations, 83–84
  bias and prejudice, 29
  board chair role, 116–17
  board composition, 112–14T
  board culture, 115–17
  code of conduct, 105–6
  collegiality, 94
  commitment considerations, 9–12
  confidentiality, 14
  conflict of interest, 14, 18–23, 115–16
  decision-making and business judgment rule, 15
  diligence, 16, 27–33
  duty of care, 15–16
  dysfunction, 117
  expectations, 11–12
  experience, 9, 179

external vs internal, 22–23, 112, 115–16
faculty representation, 163
fiduciary duty, 13–17, 103, 105–6
financial expertise, 179
fundraising expectations, 76–77
Indigenous, 75–76
legal duties, 13–17
management of, 115–17, 119
membership considerations, 7–12
not for own benefit, 15
policy framework, 111–12
provincial government appointees, 70–71
recruitment practices, 71
roles and responsibilities, 13–17, 28–29, 98–99, 100, 102, 105–6
stakeholder appointees, 117
student representation, 163
tenure appointments authority, 54–55T, 56
true purpose, 15
University culture and concepts, 90–106. *See also* Universities
  academic, 90–91
  academic freedom, 98–102
  advancement of knowledge, 91
  bicameral governance, 95–98
  collegiality, 94
  commons, 91
  freedom of expression (speech), 103–6
  governance models, 95–96
  institutional autonomy, 91–94
  unionization, 96–98
University finances, 179–89. *See also* Universities
  budget process and decisions, 186–88
  donors, 76–78, 183
  expenditures, 184, 185, 188
  financial trends, 184–86, 188–89
  fixed share grant funding, 180
  funding statistics, 181–82
  government funding, 179–81, 182–83, 184
  losses, 182
  metrics categories, 181
  performance-based funding model, 69–70, 181
  revenue, 34, 182–83, 184, 186, 187

student financial aids, 187
surpluses, 185
tuition revenue, 34, 183, 184, 186, 187
University governance professionals, 16–17, 64, 167–68, 192
University governance structure, 109–19. *See also* University board governance
   academic governing body composition, 118T–19T
   board composition, 112–14T
   board management of internal members, 115–17
   legislation and bylaws, 109–11
   policies, 111–12
University of British Columbia (UBC)
   board of governors, 104–5
   faculty association, 104–5
   freedom of expression (speech) vs academic freedom, 104–5
   human resources, 60n1
   president resignation, 104–5
University of Calgary (AB)
   administration, 65
   autonomy vs donor interference, 77
   board composition, 113T–14T
University of Ontario Institute of Technology (ON)
   board composition, 113T–14T
   tenure legislation, 55T
University of Ontario Institute of Technology Act (2002), 22–23, 79n9, 159n1
University of Prince Edward Island, 62n5

University of Saskatchewan
   tenure legislation, 55T
   tricameral governance, 95–96
University of Toronto (ON)
   administration, 65
   anti-Black racism, 29n1
   faculty appointments and political interference, 92, 92n6
   human resources, 60n1
   institutional autonomy, 92
   unicameral governance, 95, 95n19
University of Waterloo (ON)
   board composition, 113T–14T
University of Waterloo Act
   academic governing body powers, 146T–58T
   governing board powers, 123, 127T–45T
   shared governance, 160
University of Western Ontario (ON), 40
University of Winnipeg (MB) Act
   academic governing body powers, 146T–58T
   governing board powers, 123, 127T–45T
   shared governance, 160
University secretary, 16–17, 64
Usher, Alex, 8, 41–42, 186, 188

Walton, Gerald, 53
Weingarten, Harvey, 51–52
Women (faculty), 49–51

York University (ON), 87n17

About the Author

Cheryl Foy believes that good governance is foundational to organizational effectiveness. She has worked in governance for twenty years, having held general counsel and corporate secretary executive roles with public and private technology companies and at two Ontario universities. She is currently university secretary and general counsel at Ontario Tech University. She also acts as the university's chief Privacy, Compliance and Risk Officer. She is a published writer and is currently writing a column on ethics for *Canadian Lawyer InHouse* and a column called "Legally Speaking" for *University Affairs* magazine. In support of her governance work, Ms. Foy provides additional information and resources on her website at: www.universitygovernance.ca. She was awarded the Women's Law Association of Ontario General Counsel Award in 2020 for her leadership and her commitment to the success of women in law.

Ms. Foy is an advocate for good governance and the development of the in-house legal profession. She is a founder and the past president of Women General Counsel Canada, a national organization established by female general counsel who recognize that the role of general counsel is a unique leadership role bridging law and business and also that women in the general counsel role have common challenges and opportunities. She has served on a number of boards and currently serves as investment committee chair and board member for the Canadian Universities Reciprocal Insurance Exchange.

Ms. Foy holds an honours bachelor of arts degree in political studies and a bachelor of laws, from Queen's University at Kingston, Ontario, and was called to the Ontario bar in 1995.